816-589-3559

HOME DECORATING
with ORIGAMI

TOMOKO FUSE

JAPAN PUBLICATIONS TRADING COMPANY

© 2000 by Tomoko Fuse
Illustrations by Yasuo Aizawa
Photographs by Tokuko Yasui

Published by Japan Publications Trading Co., Ltd.,
1-2-1 Sarugaku-cho, Chiyoda-ku, Tokyo, 101-0064 Japan.

First edition, First printing: September 2000

Distributors:
United States: Kodansha America, Inc. through Oxford University Press,
198 Madison Avenue, New York, NY 10016.
Canada: Fitzhenry & Whiteside Ltd.,
195 Allstate Parkway, Markham, Ontario L3R 4T8.
United Kingdom and Europe: Premier Book Marketing Ltd.,
Clarendon House, 52, Cornmarket Street, Oxford OX1 3HJ, England.
Australia and New Zealand: Bookwise International,
54 Crittenden Road, Findon, South Australia 5023, Australia.
Asia and Japan: Japan Publications Trading Co., Ltd.,
1-2-1 Sarugaku-cho, Chiyoda-ku, Tokyo, 101-0064 Japan.

ISBN 4-88996-059-7

Printed in Japan

Contents

Preface

This book features a wealth of origami suitable for happy events and occasions of celebration. Some are good for keeping by your side and decorating your room with your own ideas.

You will find it delightful to choose colorful paper and think about the combination, imagining the reactions of those who see the work or those who receive it as a present. You will feel a little thrill when you get to work on it. A warm smile will break over you face when you hear someone says, "Please show me how to make it?" or "Thank you. I copied your model."

It is also a good diversion for you to fold paper for your own purpose. I sincerely hope that this book will brighten you life and give you a happy smile.

March 10, 2000
Tomoko Fuse

Symbols and Folding Techniques

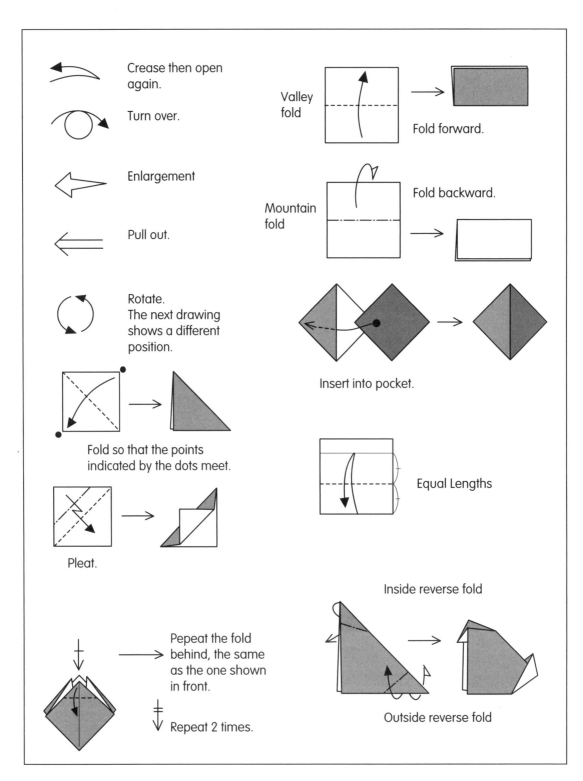

Crease then open again.

Turn over.

Enlargement

Pull out.

Rotate.
The next drawing shows a different position.

Fold so that the points indicated by the dots meet.

Pleat.

Pepeat the fold behind, the same as the one shown in front.

Repeat 2 times.

Valley fold

Fold forward.

Mountain fold

Fold backward.

Insert into pocket.

Equal Lengths

Inside reverse fold

Outside reverse fold

6

Mr. Yujiro Muraue
-2-1 Sarugaku-cho,
.ku,

LETTER HOLDERS; 1, 2, 3, 4, 5 (pages 24~31)

CARD 3 (page 36) with Stopper HEART (p. 44)

CARD 3 with Stoppers CRANE(p.38), PEACH(p.42), CARNATION(p.41), SAILBOAT(p.46),
CHURCH(p.42), IRIS(p.38) with clockwise

CARD 1(p.32), CARD 2(p.34)

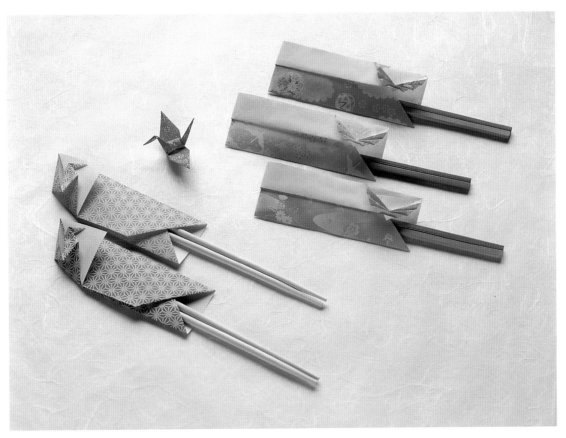

CHOPSTICK CASES with CRANE(p.50) & BUTTERFLY(p.51)

CHOPSTICK RESTS; Fan(p.52), V-shape(p.64)

FLOWER VASE COVERS; 1(p.54), Variation C of Spring-like Cover(p.61)

FLOWER VASE COVERS (from left);
1(p.54), Spring-like Bottom(p.59), 2-Three sides(p.57), 2-Four sides(p.57), Spiral(p.62)

DECAGONAL STARS (from top); E(p.97), B(p.94)

TWINKLING STARS (pp.74~97)

HEXAGONAL STARS with Accessory Parts (pp.78~88)

CAKE BOXES; 1(p.100), 2(p.106)

CAKE BOXES(from left); 1-A lid of flower(p.100), 1-Plain lid(p.103)

TULIP CUPS(p.122) & PACKAGE(p.125)

PACKAGES(from left); Six sides-A(p.110), Square(a) & (b)(p.108), Six sides-B(p.112)

PACKAGES with Stoppers(pp.115~117) (from left); Trapezoid(p.120), Dice(113), Half-size Dice(p.118)

HANA(p.66)

BALALAIKA(p.69)

Chapter 1

Cards and Letter Holders

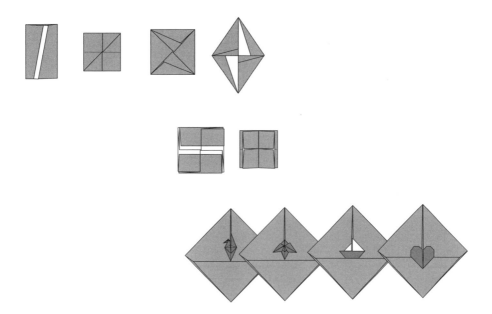

Simplicity is important.

The essential characteristic of origami may be in the act of folding paper. In applying origami to cards and letter holders, I think simple folding is best. Those who open cards and letter holders have to unfold the completed works and fold them again. It means that they have to experience for themselves what the author has gone through. If the works are complicated, it will be difficult for them to reconstruct the origami and they may be at a loss what to do.

The folding procedure must be simple. To the works you may add something that suggests the season or the object. It depends on your idea. You may write or stick what you like on them. Introduced in this chapter, there are several such ideas. Those who open the cards and letter holders will be completely satisfied with the mechanics before being struck with admiration. They surely want to try to fold them by themselves.

Letter Holder 1

(Pictured on page 7)

Appropriate paper size:
21 x 30 cm (8½ x 12") or
18 x 26 cm (7 x 10")

Step 1 is the point of this work. You may decide the folding width and angle freely as you like. It is possible to start with the edge folded as shown on the right page.

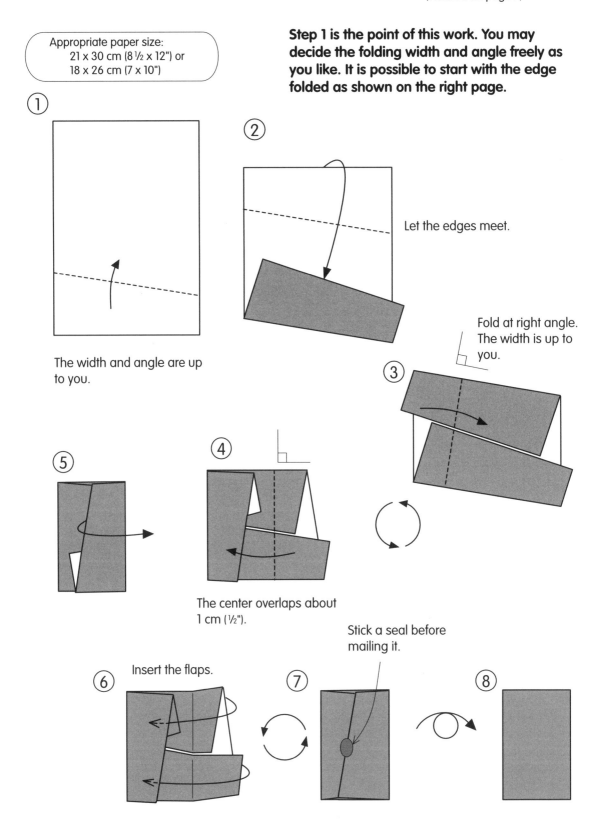

① The width and angle are up to you.

② Let the edges meet.

③ Fold at right angle. The width is up to you.

④ The center overlaps about 1 cm (½").

⑤

⑥ Insert the flaps.

⑦ Stick a seal before mailing it.

⑧

◆ Add one fold ◆

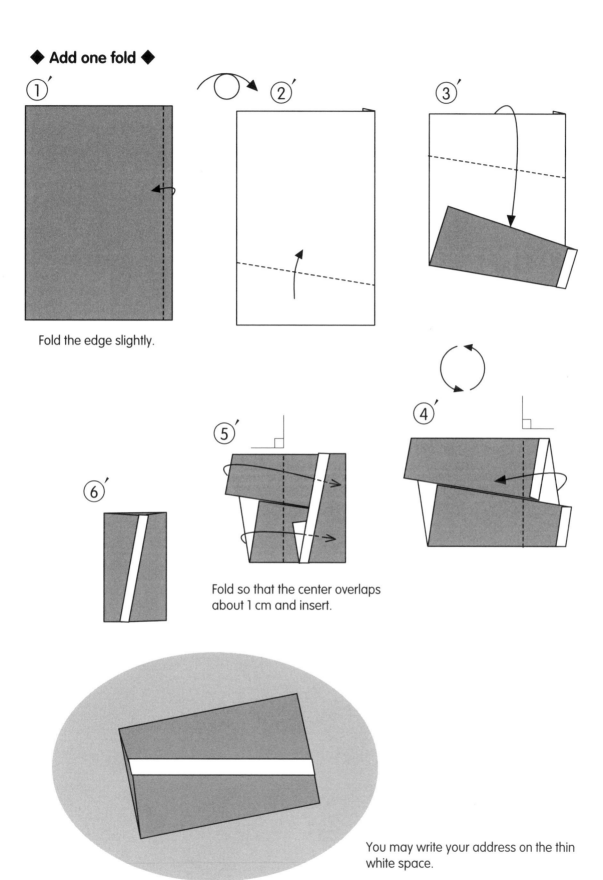

① Fold the edge slightly.

⑤ Fold so that the center overlaps about 1 cm and insert.

You may write your address on the thin white space.

25

Letter Holder 2

(Pictured on page 7)

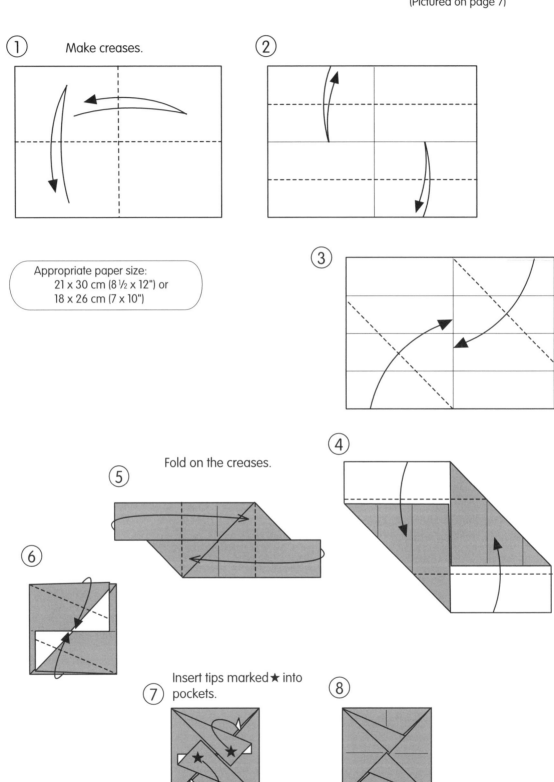

① Make creases.

②

Appropriate paper size:
21 x 30 cm (8 ½ x 12") or
18 x 26 cm (7 x 10")

③

④

⑤ Fold on the creases.

⑥

⑦ Insert tips marked ★ into pockets.

⑧

Letter Holder 3

(Pictured on page 7)

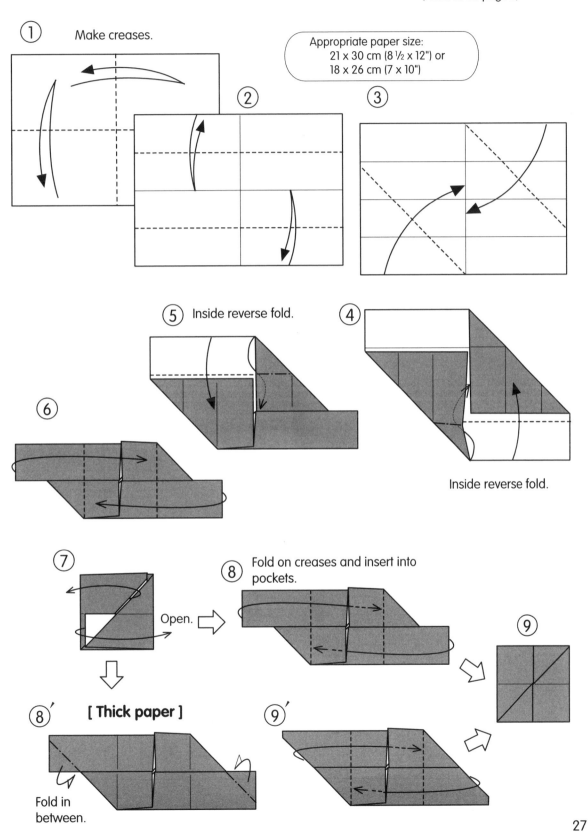

① Make creases.

Appropriate paper size:
21 x 30 cm (8 ½ x 12") or
18 x 26 cm (7 x 10")

②

③

⑤ Inside reverse fold.

④

Inside reverse fold.

⑥

⑦ Open.

⑧ Fold on creases and insert into pockets.

⑨

⑧' [Thick paper]

Fold in between.

⑨'

27

Letter Holder 4

(Pictured on page 7)

Appropriate paper size:
21 x 30 cm (8 ½ x 12") or
18 x 26 cm (7 x 10")

①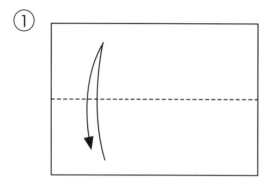

②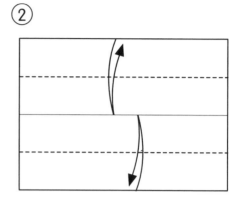

③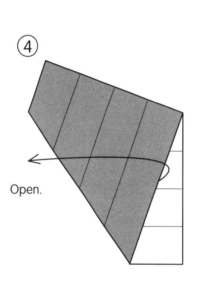

Fold ● to ● .

④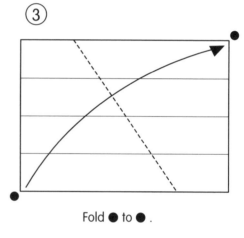

Open.

⑤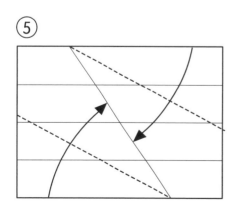

⑥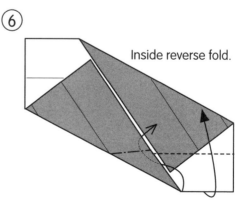

Inside reverse fold.

Mr. Yujiro Muraue
1-2-1 Sarugaku-cho,
Chiyoda-ku,
Tokyo, Japan

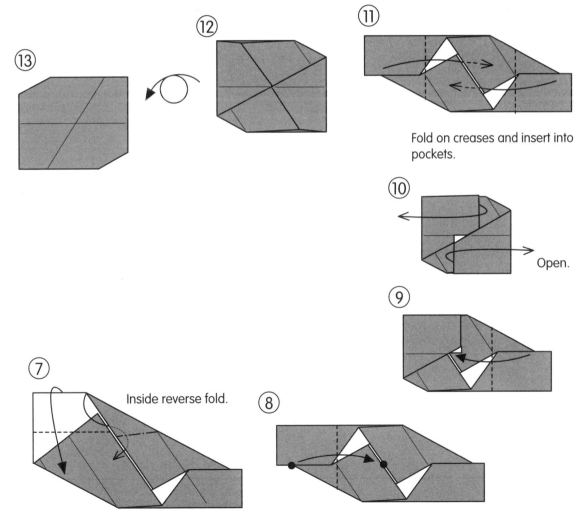

⑬

⑫

⑪

Fold on creases and insert into pockets.

⑩

Open.

⑨

⑦

Inside reverse fold.

⑧

Letter Holder 5

(Pictured on page 7)

Enjoy variations by changing steps⑧ and⑩ .

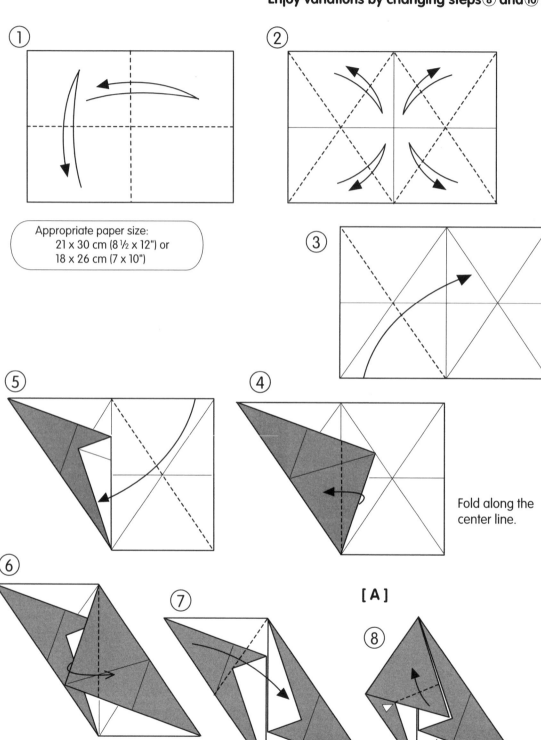

Appropriate paper size:
21 x 30 cm (8 ½ x 12") or
18 x 26 cm (7 x 10")

Fold along the
center line.

[A]

[B]

From step ⑦ on page 30.

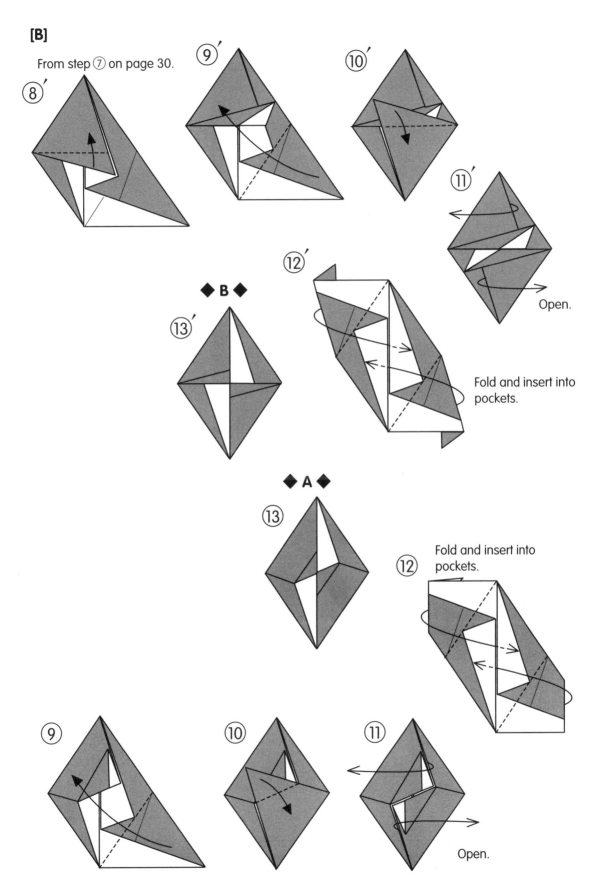

⑧'

⑨'

⑩'

⑪'

Open.

⑫'

◆ B ◆

⑬'

Fold and insert into pockets.

◆ A ◆

⑬

⑫ Fold and insert into pockets.

⑨

⑩

⑪

Open.

31

Card 1

(Pictured on page 10)

Appropriate paper size:
21 x 30 cm (8 ½ x 12") or
18 x 26 cm (7 x 10")

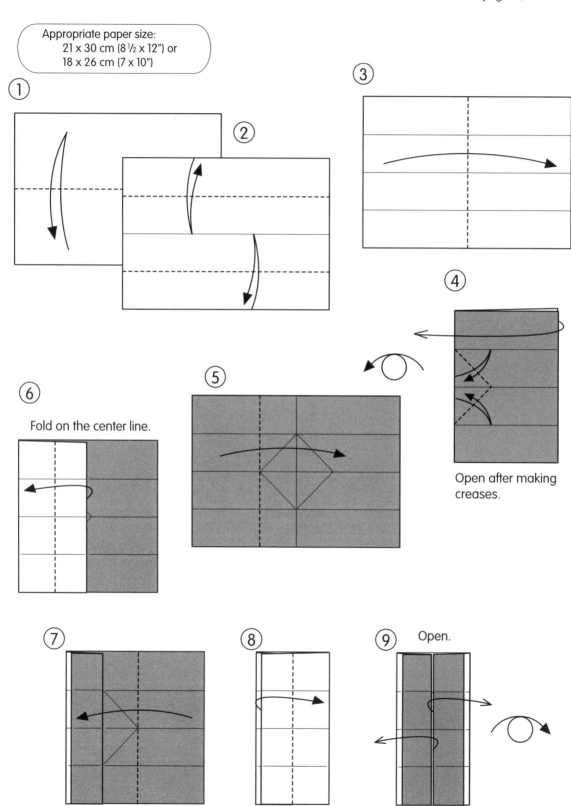

② Fold on the center line.

⑤

④ Open after making creases.

⑥ Fold on the center line.

⑦

⑧

⑨ Open.

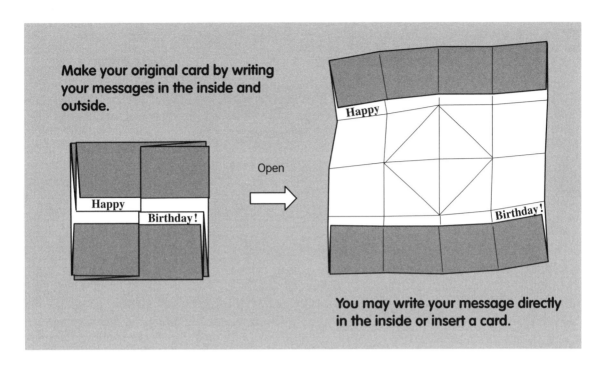

Make your original card by writing your messages in the inside and outside.

Open

Happy
Birthday!

Happy

Birthday!

You may write your message directly in the inside or insert a card.

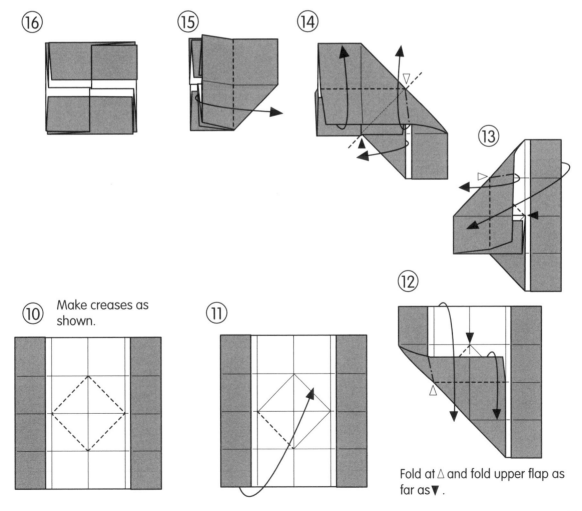

⑯

⑮

⑭

⑬

⑩ Make creases as shown.

⑪

⑫

Fold at △ and fold upper flap as far as ▼.

33

Card 2

(Pictured on page 10)

Appropriate paper size:
21 x 30 cm (8 ½ x 12") or
18 x 26 cm (7 x 10")

When opened, the inside suddenly comes out pop. You will find the opening mechanics interesting.

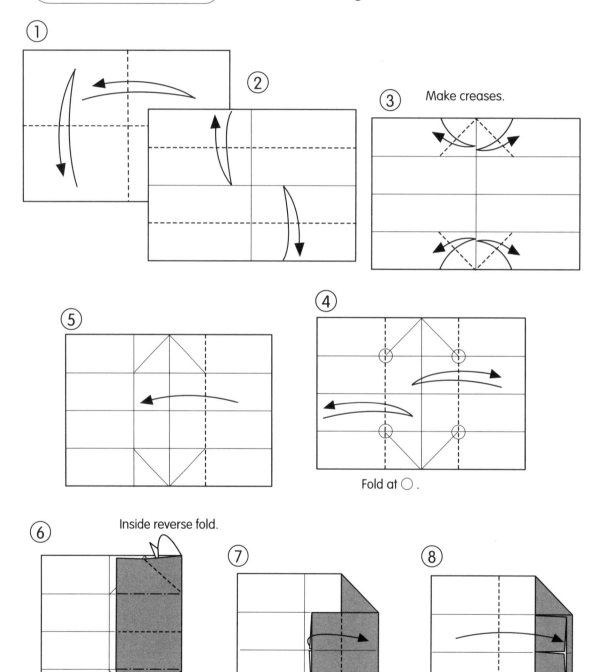

③ Make creases.

④ Fold at ◯.

⑥ Inside reverse fold.

34

⑨ Inside reverse fold.

⑩

⑪ Insert into pockets.

⑫

Pull out ○. The inside will come out pop.

Card 3

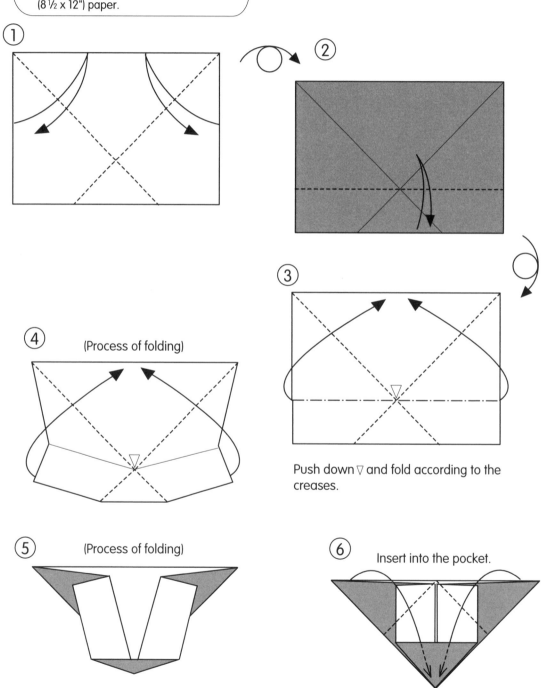

(Pictured on pages 8~9)

This card has many uses. Fix the card with a variety of stoppers to represent the season and events.

To begin with, you had better practice folding this card, using 21 cm x 30 cm (8 ½ x 12") paper.

① ②

③

④ (Process of folding)

Push down ▽ and fold according to the creases.

⑤ (Process of folding)

⑥ Insert into the pocket.

36

◆ To ensure easy opening and closing ◆

Step⑥ . When the paper is thick, it is hard to insert the tips. In that case, fold the paper, leaving a little space along the top edge.

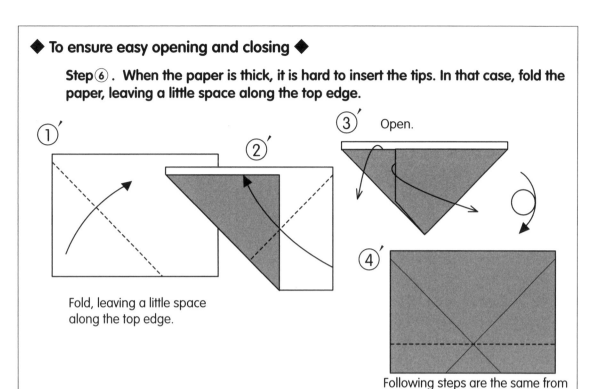

Fold, leaving a little space
along the top edge.

③′ Open.

④′

Following steps are the same from
step ③ on the left page.

A stopper of crane (see page 38)   **A stopper of heart** (see page 44)

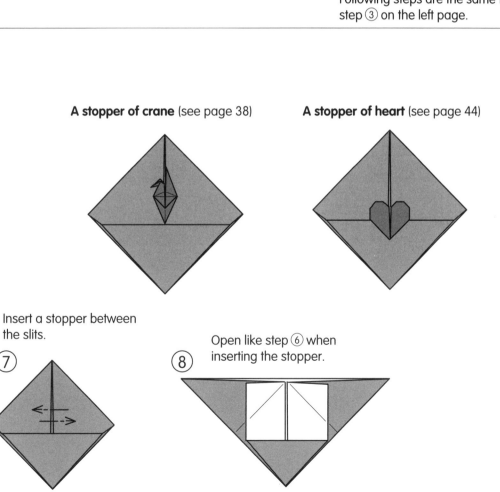

Insert a stopper between
the slits.

⑦

⑧ Open like step ⑥ when
inserting the stopper.

Stoppers Crane & Iris

(Pictured on page 9)

Stoppers for Letter holder 5. Impressions change according to different stoppers. When 21 x 30 cm (8 ½ x 12") paper is used for the card, use 7.5 x 7.5 cm (3 x 3") square paper for the stoppers.

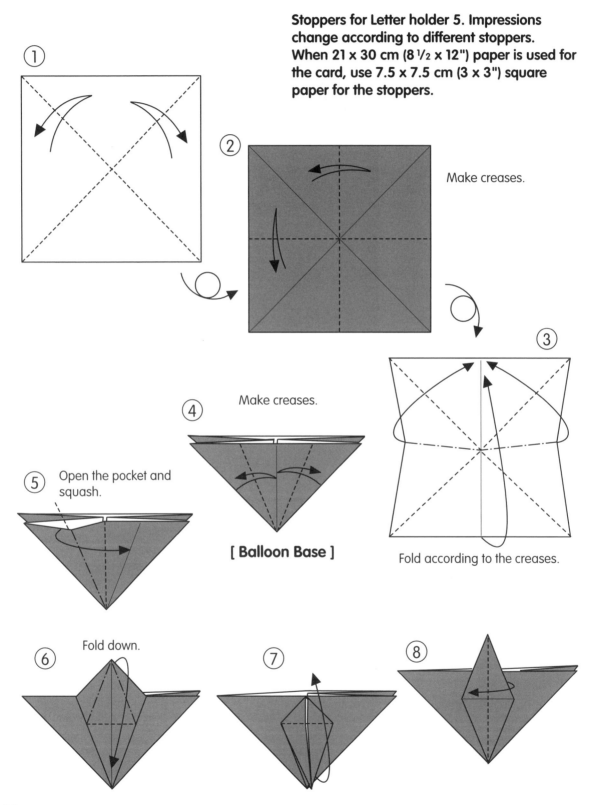

② Make creases.

④ Make creases.

[Balloon Base]

③ Fold according to the creases.

⑤ Open the pocket and squash.

⑥ Fold down.

⑦

⑧

[Another method of folding Balloon Base]

Form ④ on the left page is called 'Balloon Base.' Here is another folding method, which is traditional.

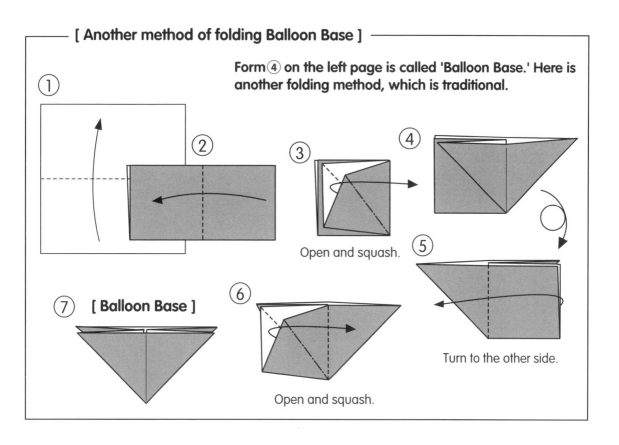

③ Open and squash.

⑤ Turn to the other side.

⑥ Open and squash.

⑦ [Balloon Base]

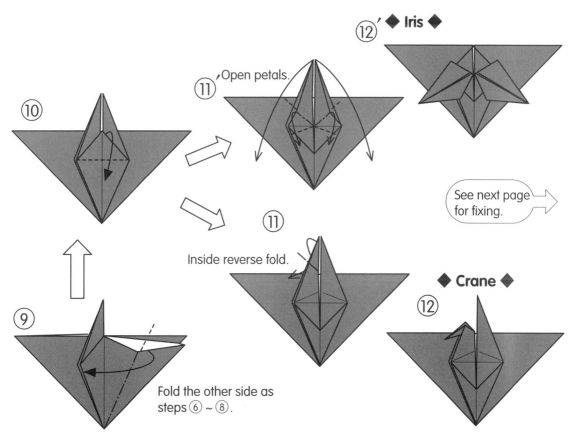

⑩

⑪ Open petals.

⑫′ ◆ Iris ◆

See next page for fixing.

⑪ Inside reverse fold.

◆ Crane ◆

⑫

⑨ Fold the other side as steps ⑥ ~ ⑧.

[How to fix]

◆ **Crane** ◆

⑧ of **Card 3** (page 37)

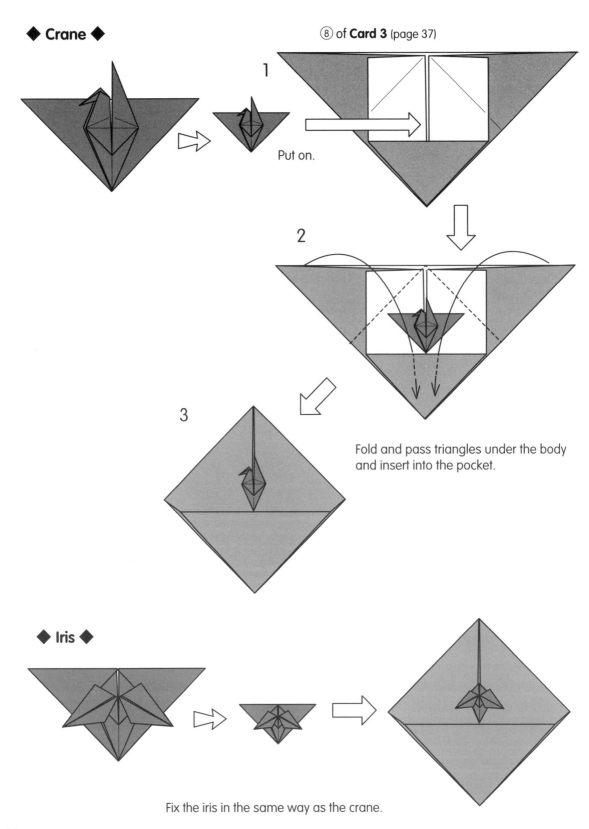

1

Put on.

2

Fold and pass triangles under the body and insert into the pocket.

3

◆ **Iris** ◆

Fix the iris in the same way as the crane.

40

Stopper **Carnation**

(Pictured on page 9)

This card is good for Mother's Day.

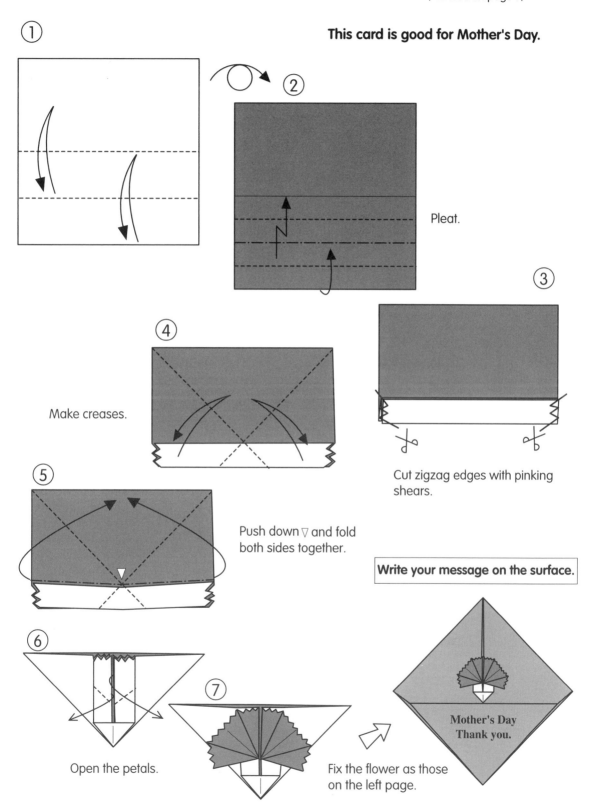

①

② Pleat.

③

④ Make creases.

Cut zigzag edges with pinking shears.

⑤ Push down ▽ and fold both sides together.

Write your message on the surface.

⑥ Open the petals.

⑦ Fix the flower as those on the left page.

Mother's Day
Thank you.

Stoppers **Peach & Church**

(Pictured on page 9)

'Peach' is suitable for someone's birthday and 'church' for Christmas. Both are applications of traditional origami.

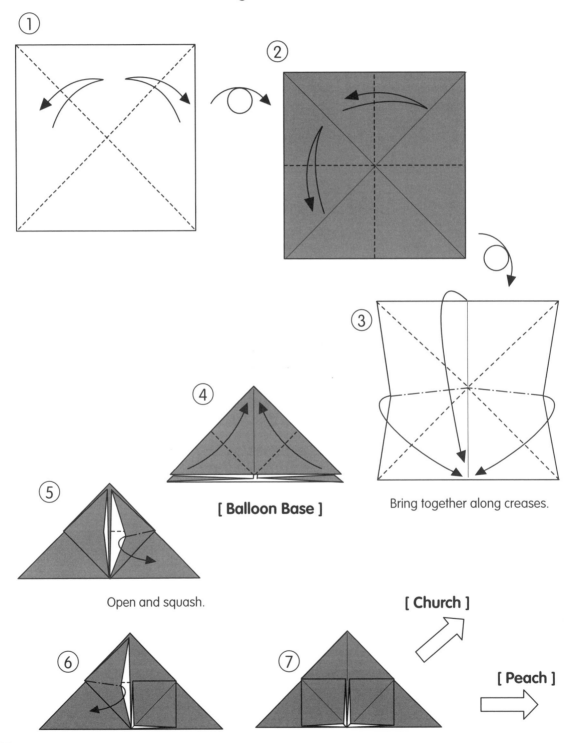

④ **[Balloon Base]**

③ Bring together along creases.

⑤ Open and squash.

⑥

⑦

[Church]

[Peach]

42

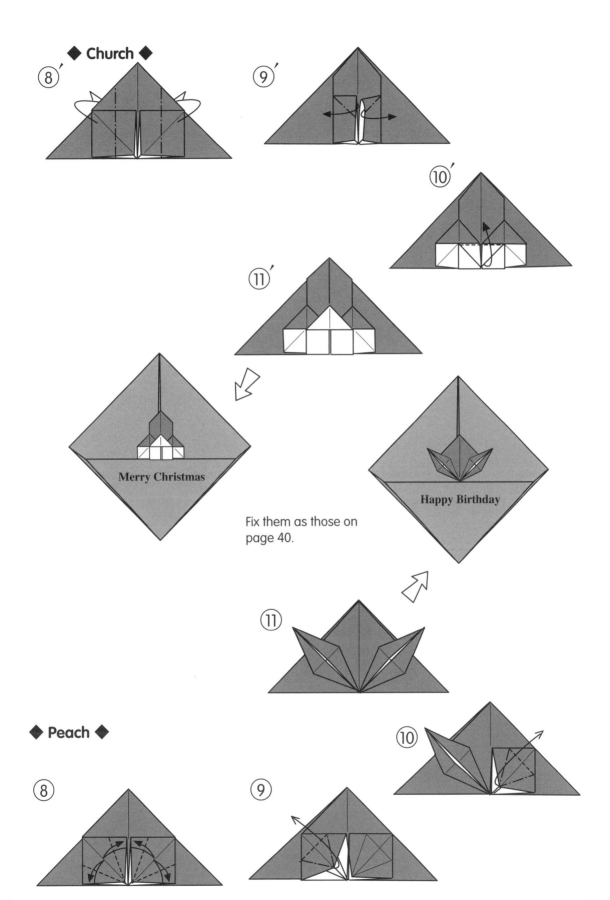

◆ Church ◆

⑧´

⑨´

⑩´

⑪´

Merry Christmas

Fix them as those on
page 40.

Happy Birthday

⑪

◆ Peach ◆

⑩

⑧

⑨

43

Stopper **Heart**

(Pictured on page 8)

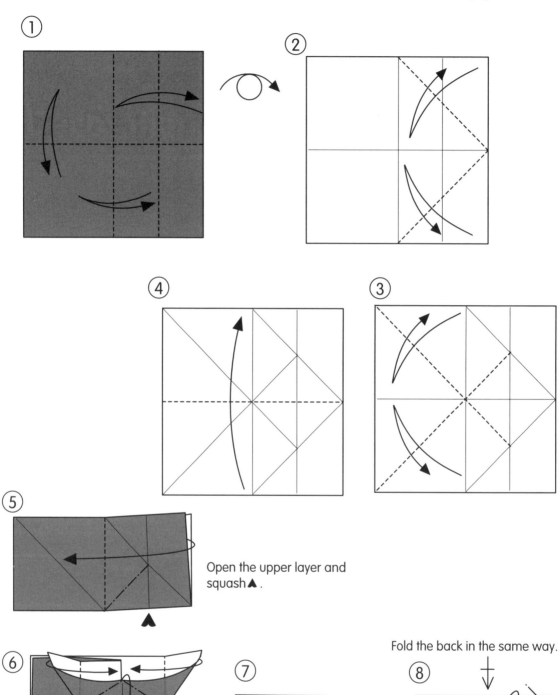

Open the upper layer and
squash ▲.

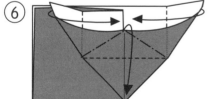

Bring down the upper layer
and fold both sides.

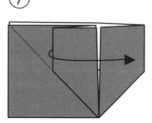

Fold the back in the same way.

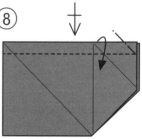

You can fix two
hearts together.

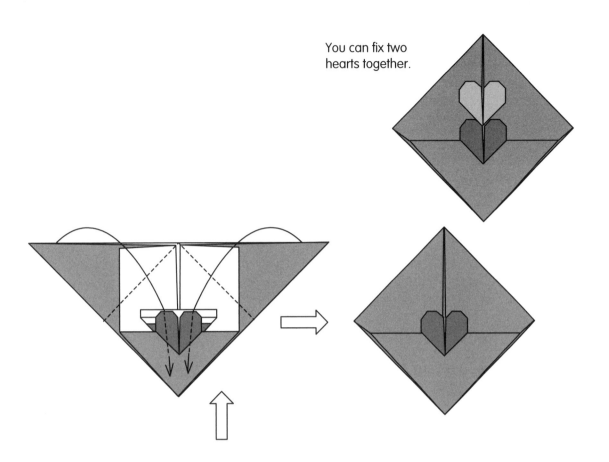

⑧ of **Card 3** (page 37)

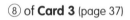

Put the heart
on the card.

⑫

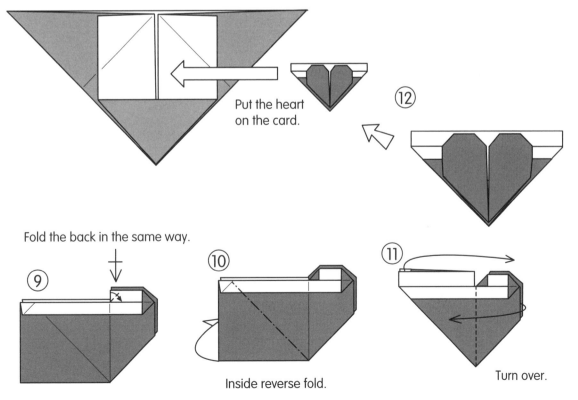

Fold the back in the same way.

⑨

⑩

Inside reverse fold.

⑪

Turn over.

Stopper **Sailboat**

(Pictured on page 9)

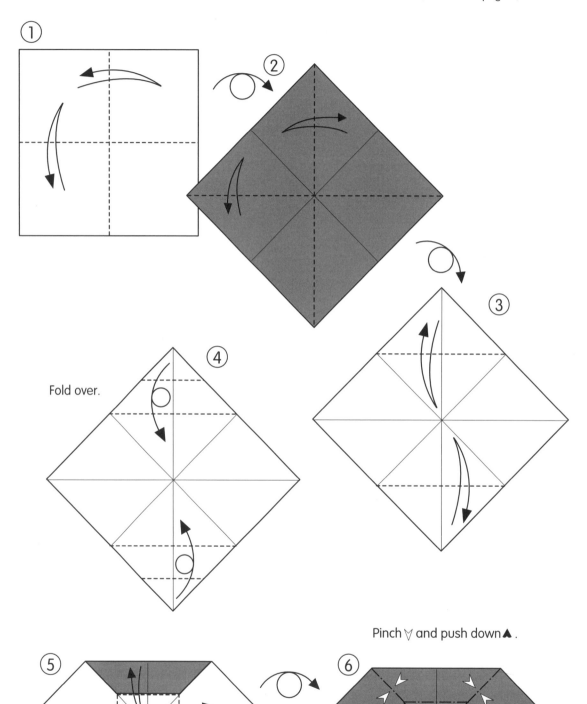

Fold over.

Pinch ⋁ and push down ▲.

46

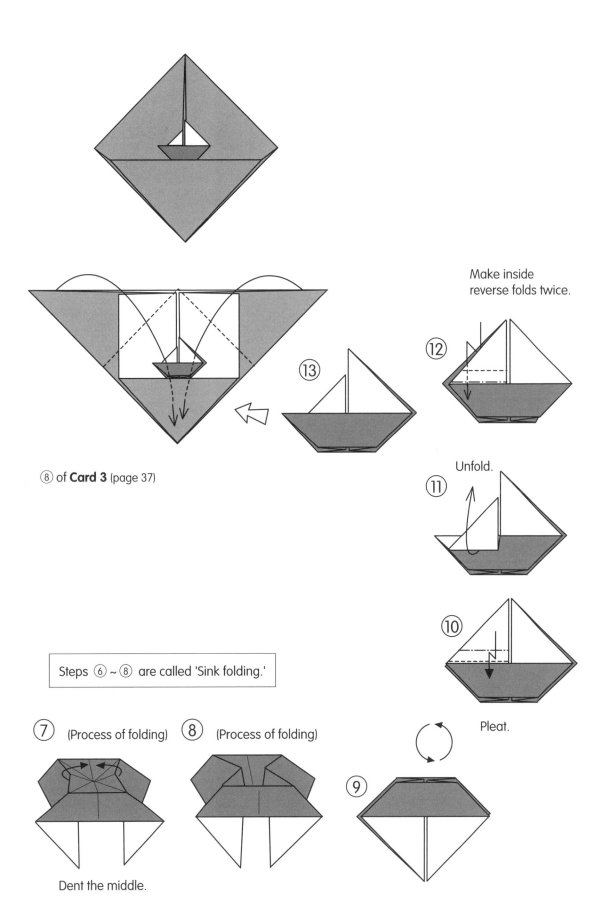

Make inside
reverse folds twice.

⑫

⑬

⑧ of **Card 3** (page 37)

Unfold.

⑪

⑩

Steps ⑥ ~ ⑧ are called 'Sink folding.'

Pleat.

⑦ (Process of folding) ⑧ (Process of folding)

⑨

Dent the middle.

A Source of Energy

There is a great difference in origami devotee's ages. Enthusiastic adult origami lovers bend all their energies to origami.

They like to teach and be taught. They give joy to other people and derive joy from what they do. When they meet difficulty in the process of folding, they have to deal with it by themselves or with the help of others. When the difficulty is cleared up, they are satisfied. 'I see,' they will say to themselves, and they feel something run through their body. It will be a kind of hormone. It will relieve you and bring a smile to your face. When you completed a superb work, something like that hormone spread through your body and a contented smile will break over your face.

Most of the origami does not require a lot of time to fold, though it depends on the work. In the course of folding this and that, the hormone exudes slowly. A little exudation of the hormone per day (not necessarily every day) will be good for the health. This will become a source of your energy.

Chapter 2

For Use and Decoration

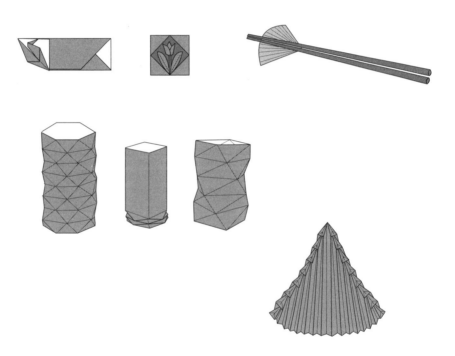

Adventure with various pieces of paper
--------- The joy of using and decorating

This chapter introduces such articles useful for our daily life as chopstick cases, coasters, and vase covers. One of the delights of origami is to make use of the folded works for practical and decorative purposes.

The material of origami is paper, so we can easily handle it. If you choose different paper, you can obtain different effect. Try to use a variety of paper, sometimes boldly choosing loud one and sometimes quiet one as the case may be.

Chopstick Case with a Crane

(Pictured on page 11)

This chopstick with a crane is suitable for a ceremonial occasion. The appropriate size of paper is 15 x 15 cm (6 x 6").

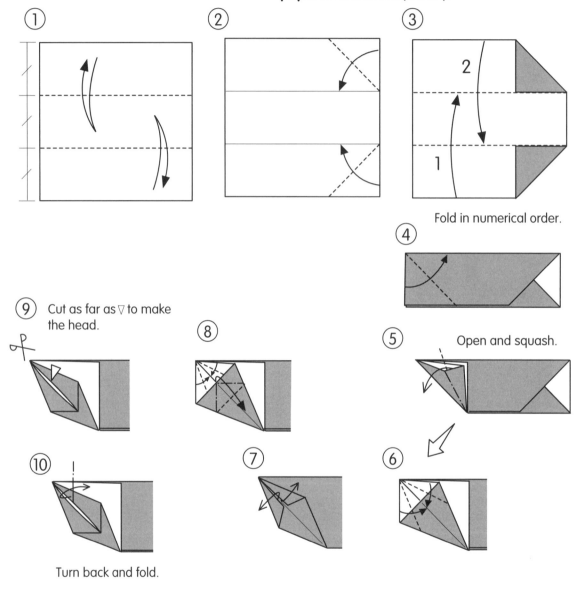

① ② ③

Fold in numerical order.

④

⑨ Cut as far as ▽ to make the head.

⑧

⑤ Open and squash.

⑦ ⑥

⑩

Turn back and fold.

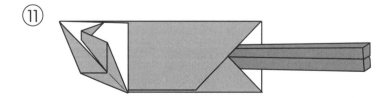

⑪

Chopstick Case with a Butterfly

(Pictured on page 11)

The appropriate paper size is 15 x 15 cm (6 x 6").

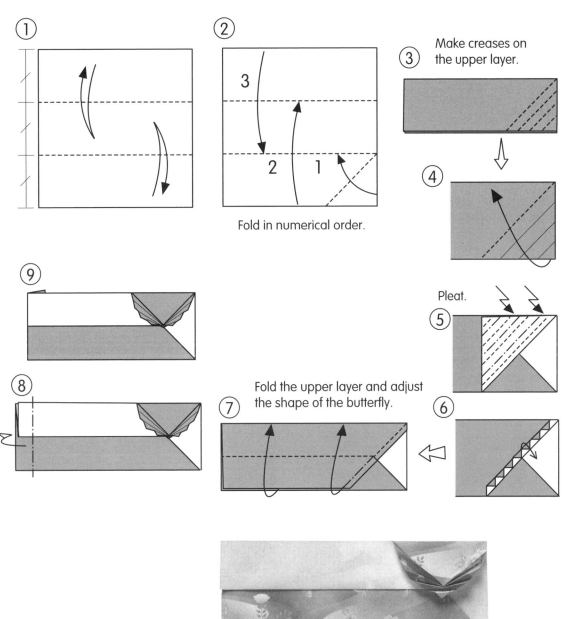

①

② Fold in numerical order.

③ Make creases on the upper layer.

④

⑤ Pleat.

⑥

⑦ Fold the upper layer and adjust the shape of the butterfly.

⑧

⑨

Chopstick Rest of a Fan

(Pictured on page 11)

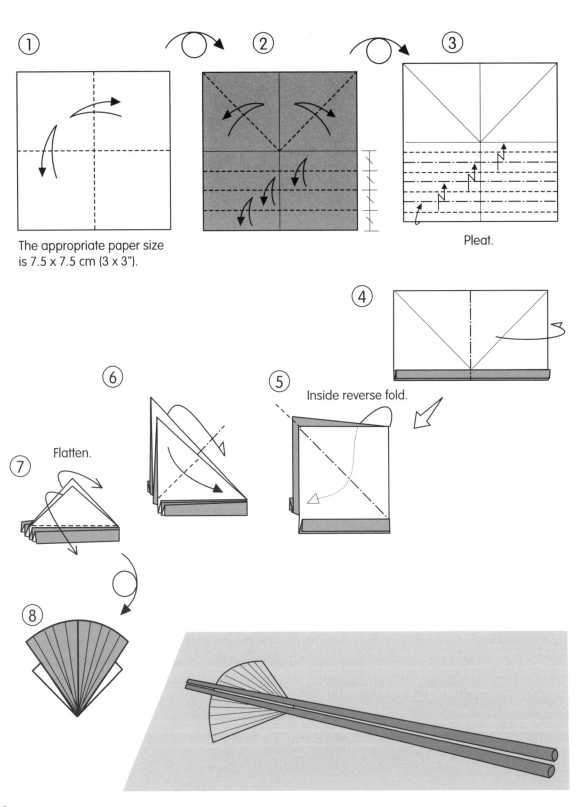

The appropriate paper size
is 7.5 x 7.5 cm (3 x 3").

Pleat.

Inside reverse fold.

Flatten.

52

Coaster of a Picture Frame

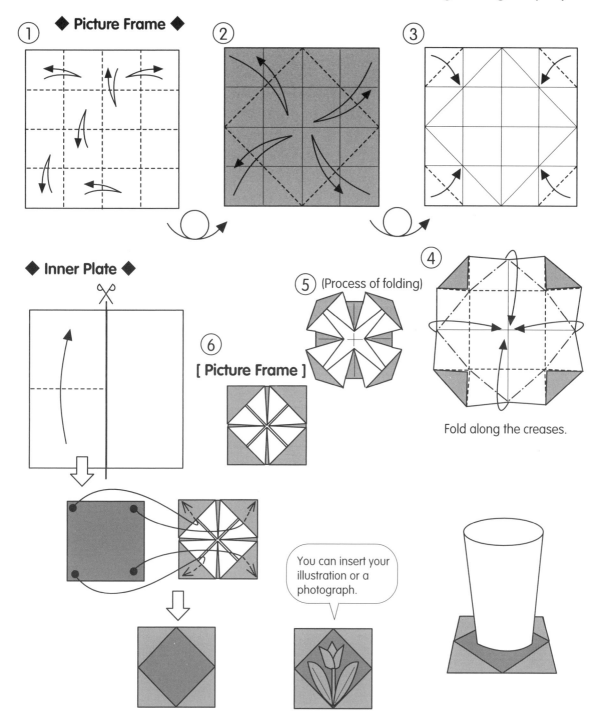

(Pictured on page 18)

Insert another paper in the 'Picture Frame' to make a coaster. It is so simple that you can make a lot of coasters easily. Put your idea into the work and arrange a delightful party.

◆ **Picture Frame** ◆

① ② ③

◆ **Inner Plate** ◆

⑤ (Process of folding)

⑥

[Picture Frame]

④

Fold along the creases.

You can insert your illustration or a photograph.

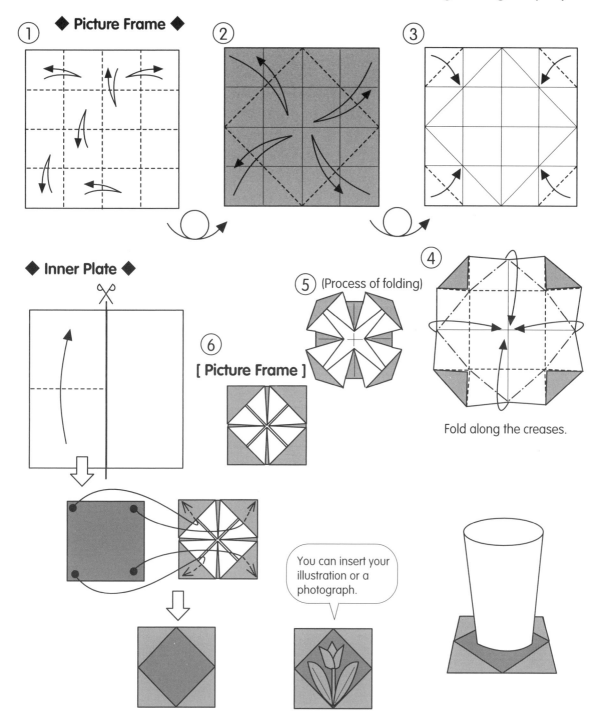

Flower Vase Cover 1

(Pictured on pages 12~13)

When arranging flowers in a glass, you can put a cover on it. Select paper and make an elegant cover like this. You had better practice folding by using 21 x 30 cm (8 ½ x 12") paper, before deciding the size and height of the cover. The method is simple and you will be familiar with it.
<u>If you use large nonflammable paper,</u> you can apply it to a lampshade.

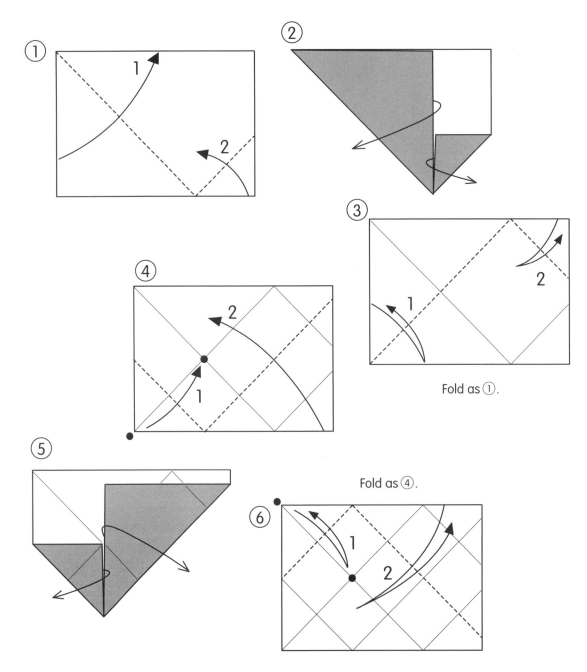

Fold as ①.

Fold as ④.

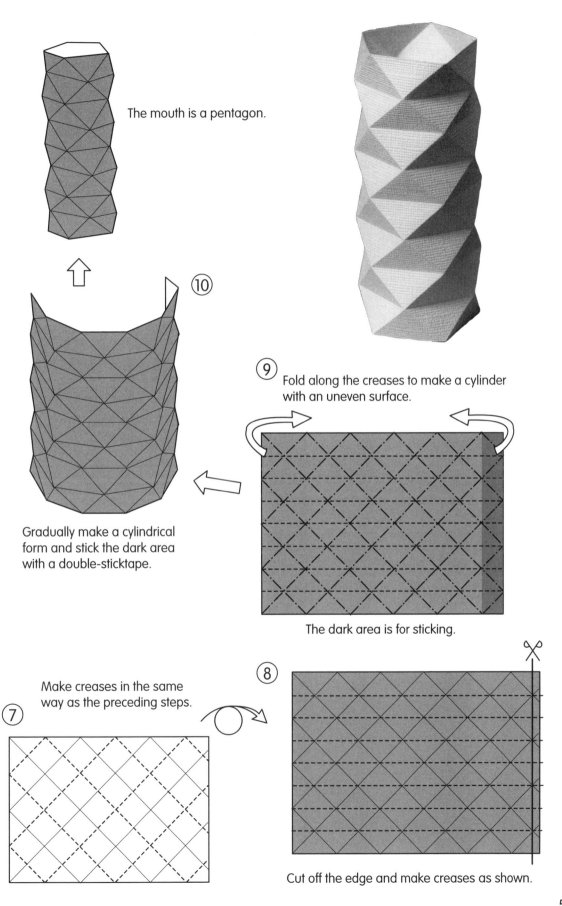

The mouth is a pentagon.

⑩

↑

Gradually make a cylindrical form and stick the dark area with a double-sticktape.

⑨ Fold along the creases to make a cylinder with an uneven surface.

The dark area is for sticking.

Make creases in the same way as the preceding steps.

⑦

⑧

Cut off the edge and make creases as shown.

55

The Size and Shape of Paper

The height and mouth shape of 'Vase Cover 1 and 2' become different according to paper sizes. As shown below, the number of triangles is equivalent to the number of sides of the mouth. If the sides of the mouth of 'Vase Cover 1' are more than seven, the surface becomes smoother, so three to six are appropriate number. If you lengthen the (h) below, you can make the vase cover higher.

Mouth with five sides

Mouth with six sides

Mouth with three sides

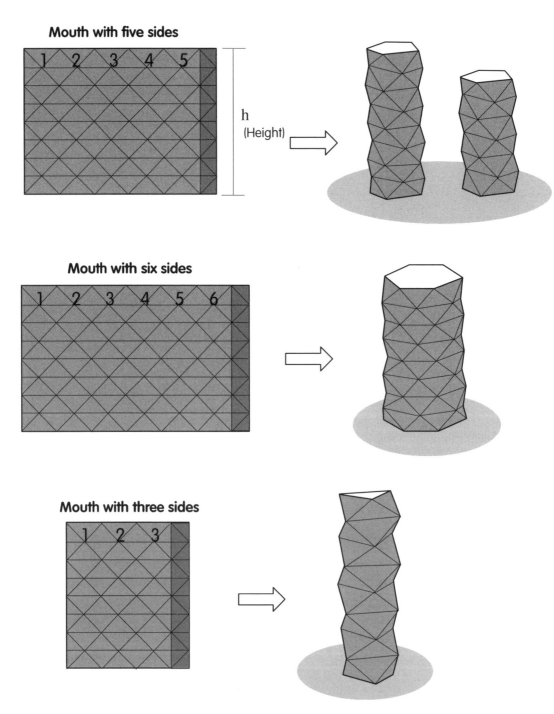

Flower Vase Cover 2

(Pictured on page 13)

This vase cover is composed of lines folded at an angle of 60 degrees. First, practice folding with 21 x 30 cm (8 ½ x 12") paper.

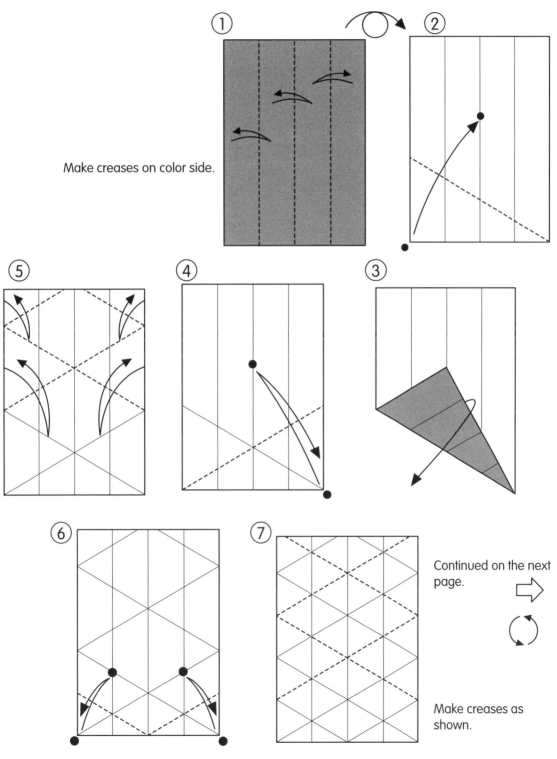

Make creases on color side.

Continued on the next page.

Make creases as shown.

57

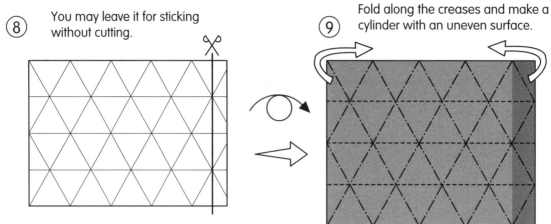

⑧ You may leave it for sticking without cutting.

⑨ Fold along the creases and make a cylinder with an uneven surface.

The dark area is for sticking.

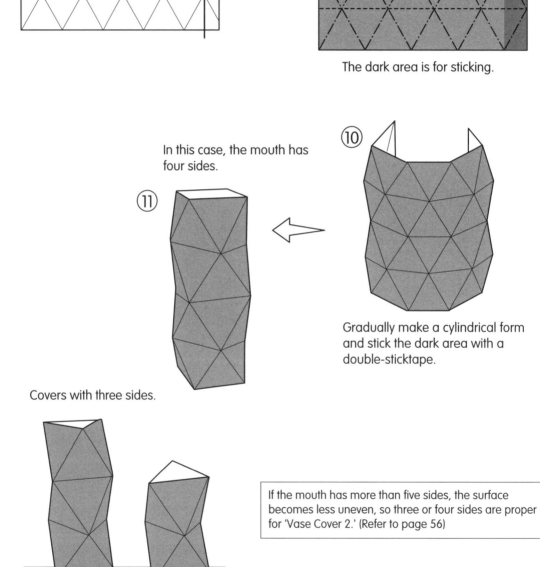

⑩ Gradually make a cylindrical form and stick the dark area with a double-sticktape.

⑪ In this case, the mouth has four sides.

Covers with three sides.

If the mouth has more than five sides, the surface becomes less uneven, so three or four sides are proper for 'Vase Cover 2.' (Refer to page 56)

Flower Vase Cover with Spring-like Bottom

(Pictured on page 13)

The vase has pleats as if it is compressed from above. You can make as many pleats as you like. It is also possible to make the pleats in the middle.
First, practice folding with 21 x 30 cm (8 ½ x 12") paper.

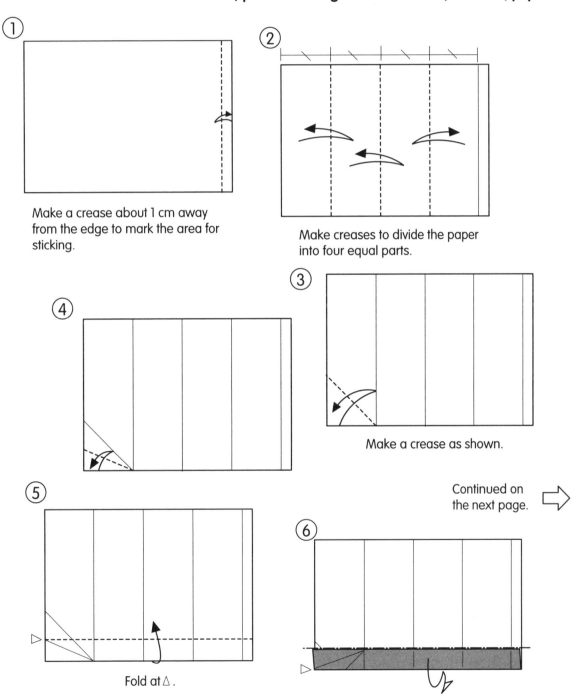

① Make a crease about 1 cm away from the edge to mark the area for sticking.

② Make creases to divide the paper into four equal parts.

③ Make a crease as shown.

④

⑤ Fold at △.

⑥ Make a crease as shown.

Continued on the next page. ⇨

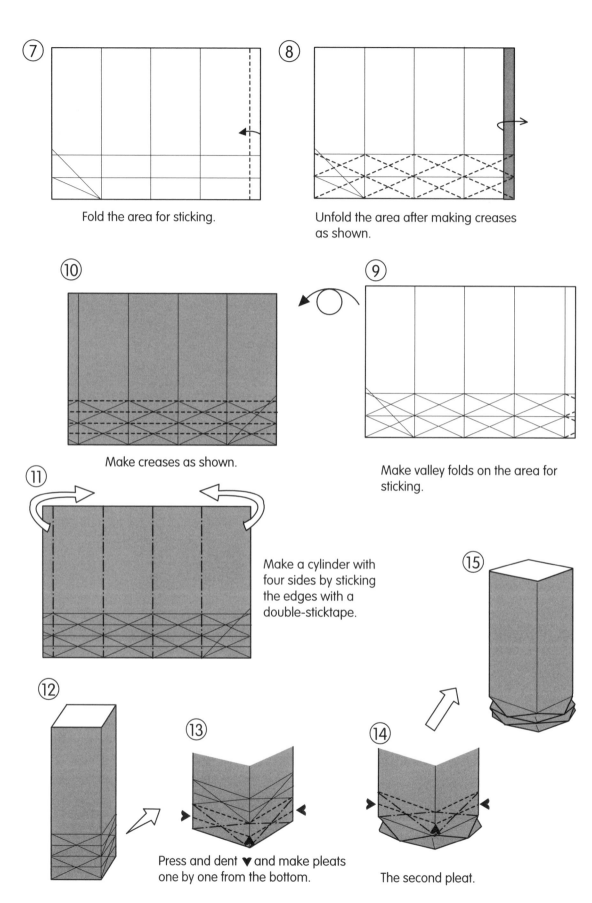

⑦ Fold the area for sticking.

⑧ Unfold the area after making creases as shown.

⑩ Make creases as shown.

⑨ Make valley folds on the area for sticking.

⑪ Make a cylinder with four sides by sticking the edges with a double-sticktape.

⑫

⑬ Press and dent ▼ and make pleats one by one from the bottom.

⑭ The second pleat.

⑮

Variations of Spring-like Cover

◆ **A** ◆ Increase the number of pleats.

◆ **B** ◆ Increase the number of pleats.

◆ **C** ◆ Make pleats in the middle.

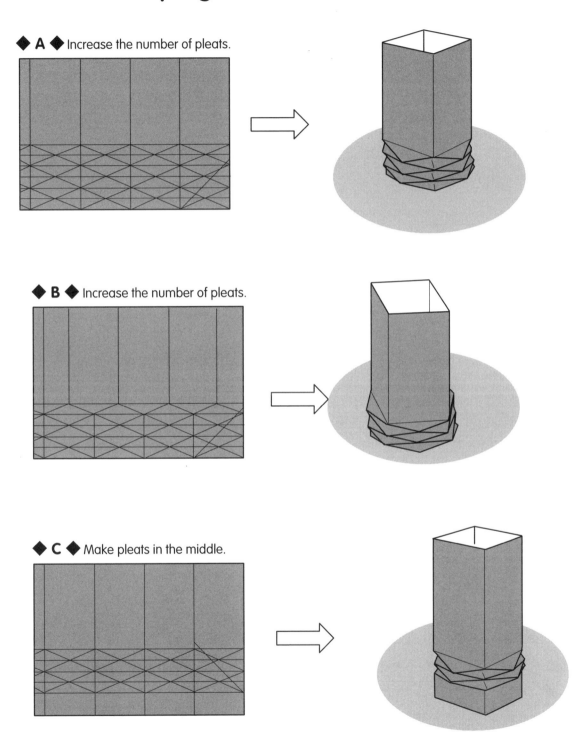

Spiral Flower Vase Cover

(Pictured on page 13)

It will be wonderful to use this vase as an objet d'art instead of flower vase cover.
Once you mastered the folding method, try to make a vase of your own, adjusting the
size and height, as you desire.
First, practice folding with 21 x 30 cm (8 ½ x 12") paper.

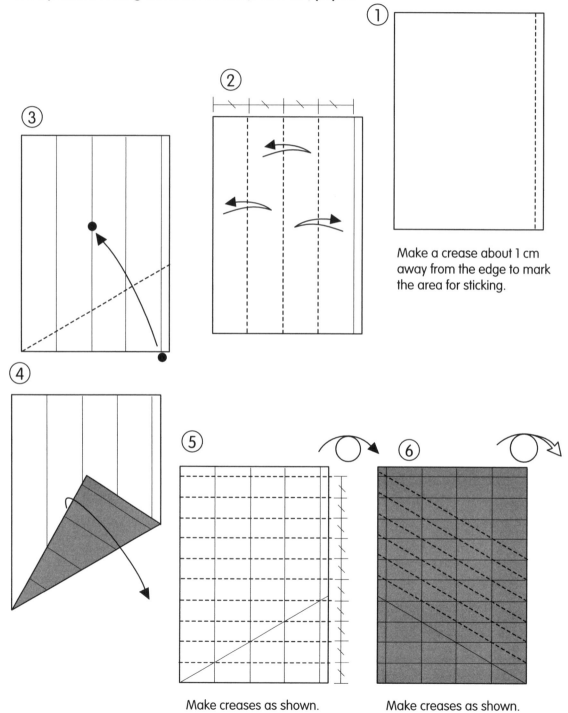

Make a crease about 1 cm
away from the edge to mark
the area for sticking.

Make creases as shown.

Make creases as shown.

⑩

Gradually make a cylindrical form and stick the edges with a double-sticktape.

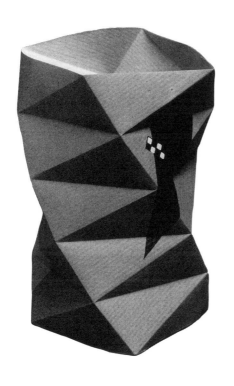

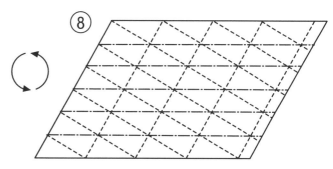

⑨

⑦ Cut the paper in the shape of a rhombus.

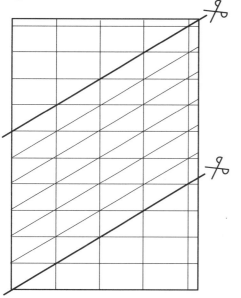

⑧

Fold along the creases to make a cylinder with an uneven surface.

63

V-shape Chopstick Rest

(Pictured on page 11)

The method of this chopstick rest will be useful for preparing 'HANA' on page 66 and 'Balalaika' on page 69.
You can make a proper size of rest from 6 x 6 cm (2 ½ x 2 ½") paper.

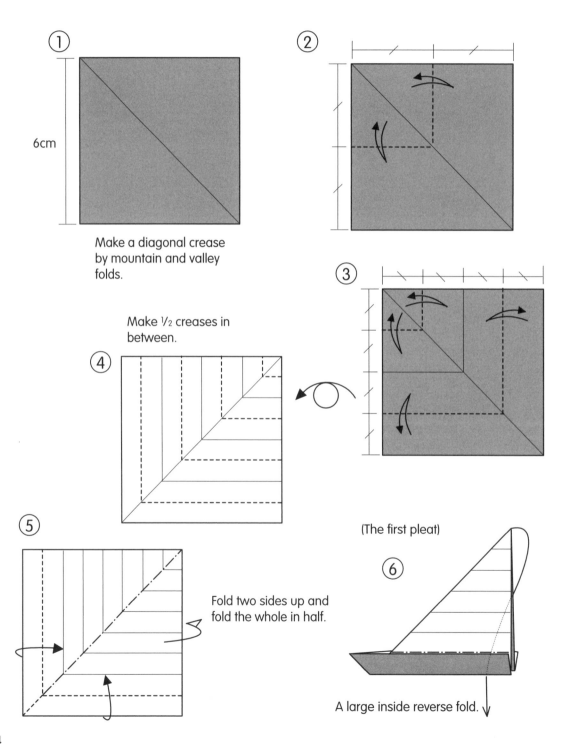

① 6cm
Make a diagonal crease by mountain and valley folds.

②

Make ½ creases in between.

③

④

⑤
Fold two sides up and fold the whole in half.

(The first pleat)
⑥
A large inside reverse fold.

64

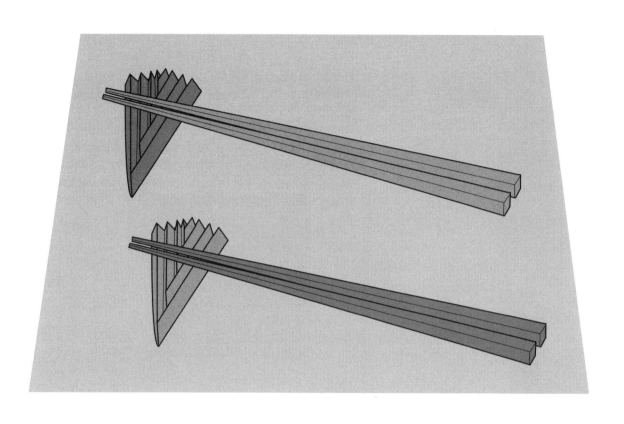

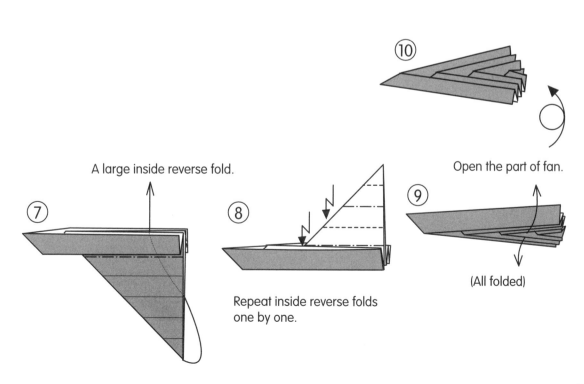

⑩

Open the part of fan.

A large inside reverse fold.

⑦

⑧

Repeat inside reverse folds
one by one.

⑨

(All folded)

HANA

(Pictured on page 21)

①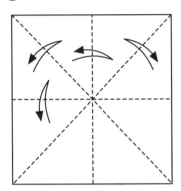

This is an abstract flower.
The method of 'V-Shape Chopstick Rest' on page 64 is applied to the four corners.
Practice with 15 x 15 cm (6 x 6") paper. When you are accustomed to this method, double the pleats and make them thinner as shown in the box on the right page. The work will become more gorgeous. Even when using large paper, thinner pleats look better.

②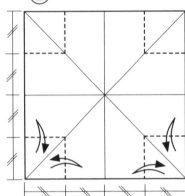

③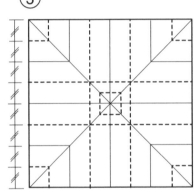

Make creases as shown.

④ Make creases as shown.

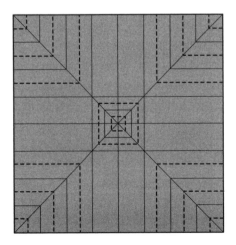

⑤ Pinch the four corners and raise the center square like a table.

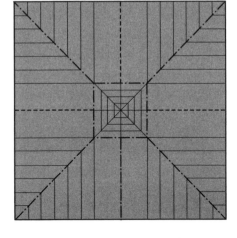

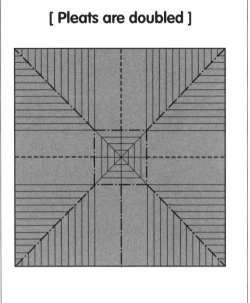

[Pleats are doubled]

Hold sides crosswise as shown
and gradually open, changing
the hold.

⑨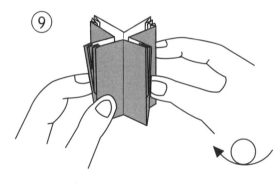

⑧ Pleat the other parts in the
same way.

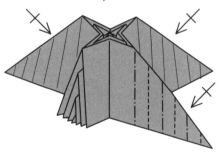

Pleat the center along the
creases and sink.

⑥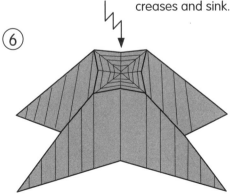

⑦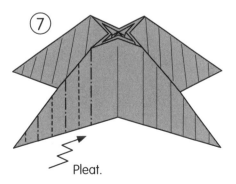

Pleat.

67

The Idea and Joy of Origami

I released this 'HANA' in a magazine long ago. Four years after the publication, I gave an exhibition of my own works at the Ueda-sozo hall and taught this 'HANA' at the class. I told the students that it would be possible to make 'HANA' with five and six sides besides the four-side one. One of the students then surprised me by telling me that she had already made beautiful 'HANA' with five, six and eight sides. I was surprised again when I received the photographs of the works that had been sent several days later.

They were original 'HANA' layered with different sizes of paper. They were unimaginably beautiful. The idea and joy of origami are thus limitless.

HANA with four layers

The pleat is doubled. (Box on page 67)
The sizes of paper: 24 cm (9 ½"), 21 cm (8 ¼"), 18 cm (7"), 15 cm (6")

Balalaika

(Pictured on page 22)

It is interesting as an objet d'art.
<u>If you employ nonflammable materials</u>, it will be used a lampshade. It will be difficult to fold the 'Balalaika' for the first time, so start with 15 x 15 cm (6 x 6") paper for practice. Later you may join the two pieces for 'Balalaika.'

◆ **Practice** ◆ 15 x 15 cm (6 x 6") paper

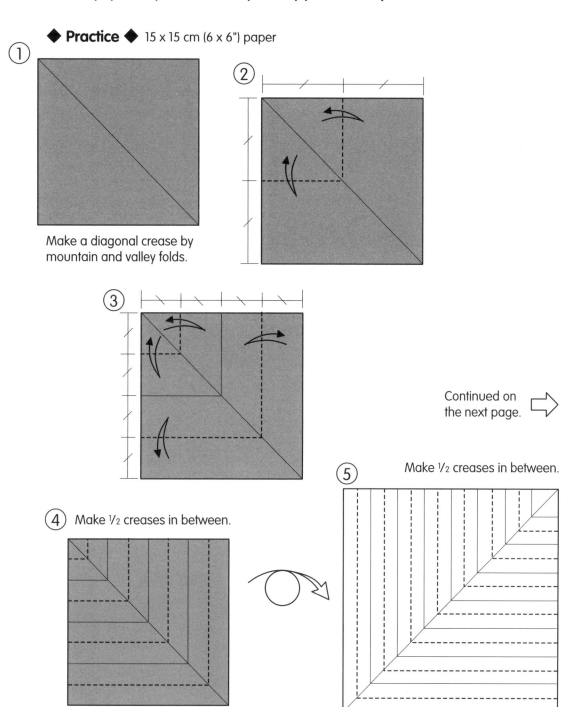

① Make a diagonal crease by mountain and valley folds.

④ Make ½ creases in between.

⑤ Make ½ creases in between.

Continued on the next page. ⇨

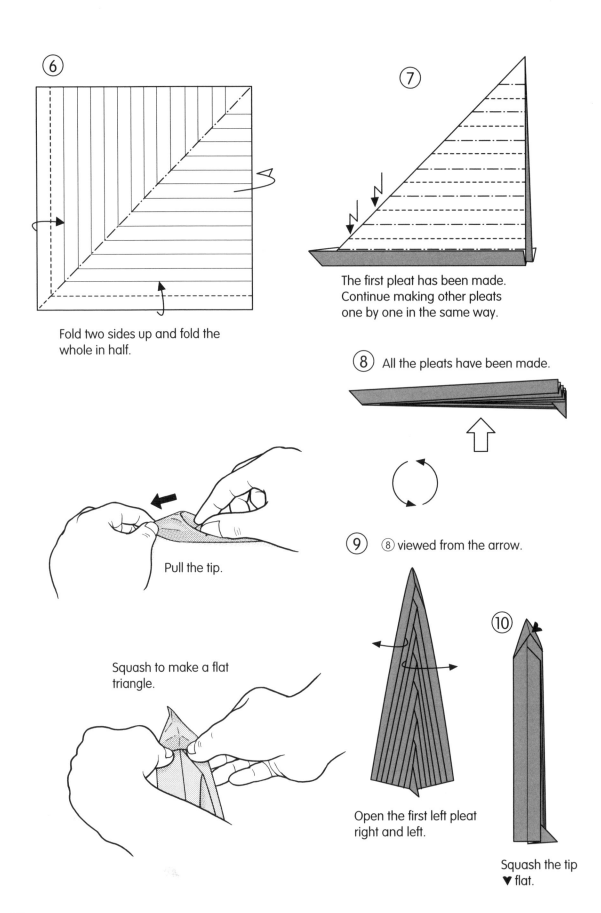

⑥ Fold two sides up and fold the whole in half.

⑦ The first pleat has been made. Continue making other pleats one by one in the same way.

⑧ All the pleats have been made.

Pull the tip.

⑨ ⑧ viewed from the arrow.

Open the first left pleat right and left.

Squash to make a flat triangle.

⑩ Squash the tip ▼ flat.

[Unfolded Balalaika]

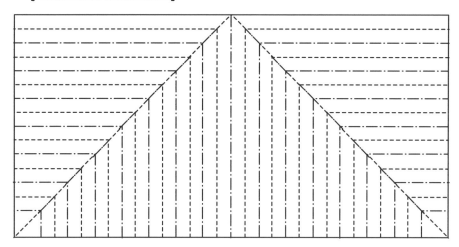

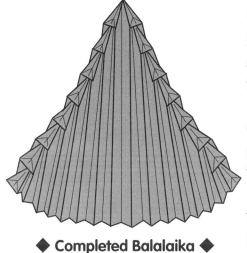

◆ **Completed Balalaika** ◆

'Balalaika' is made from rectangular paper that is as large as two pieces of square paper, and it is the same as two ⑭ of practice are joined. Fold flat and then open.

 It may be used as an objet d'art as it is. When using as a lampshade, glue the bottom of the back to prevent the leakage of light and make a hole on top for air.

 Once you have mastered the method, try to double the pleats as on the following page. When using paper larger than 30 cm (12"), it would be better to double the pleats.

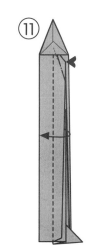

⑪

Squash the second tip flat.

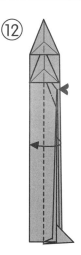

⑫

Squash the other tips in order.

⑬

Fold in the tip.

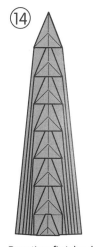

⑭

Practice finished.

The Beauty of Lines

You can make lines easily by 'folding.' The main constituent of origami is lines. A set of them, sometimes curved or spiraled, produces the characteristic beauty.

I think it is something that is induced or found out rather than artificially produced. That will be the reason why the model with outstanding lines seems light, though it looks complicated.

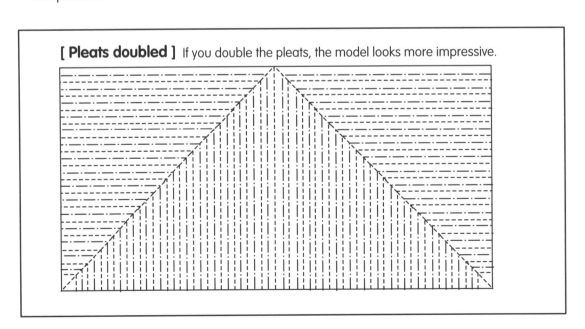

[**Pleats doubled**] If you double the pleats, the model looks more impressive.

Chapter 3

Twinkling Stars

The Wonder of Combination
--------- What does it look like?

Some origami is intended to duplicate the shape of an object faithfully, while other traditional origami does not assume concrete shape and relies on the imagination of viewers. Mr. Seiji Nishikawa emphasized the importance of this imagination. For instance, those who do not know 'fukusuke' (a popular toy in the shape of a dwarf with a big head) will imagine a different object when they see the shape. In the case of traditional Spanish origami, 'pajalita (bow tie),' it is said that it suggests a small bird.

In this chapter, I introduced units of stars that have flat shapes. Each model is interesting respectively, but if you attach some other parts it will become gorgeous.

Here is the wonder of combination, which only unit origami has. If you use proper paper, you can make fireworks, flowers and snow crystals. Some models can be used for ornaments of Christmas and the Star Festival and as decorations and accessories of wrapper. Use your imagination.

Pentagonal Star

(Pictured on page 15)

This star consists of five units. Slight errors in folding are unavoidable, but the units will be perfectly assembled in the end.

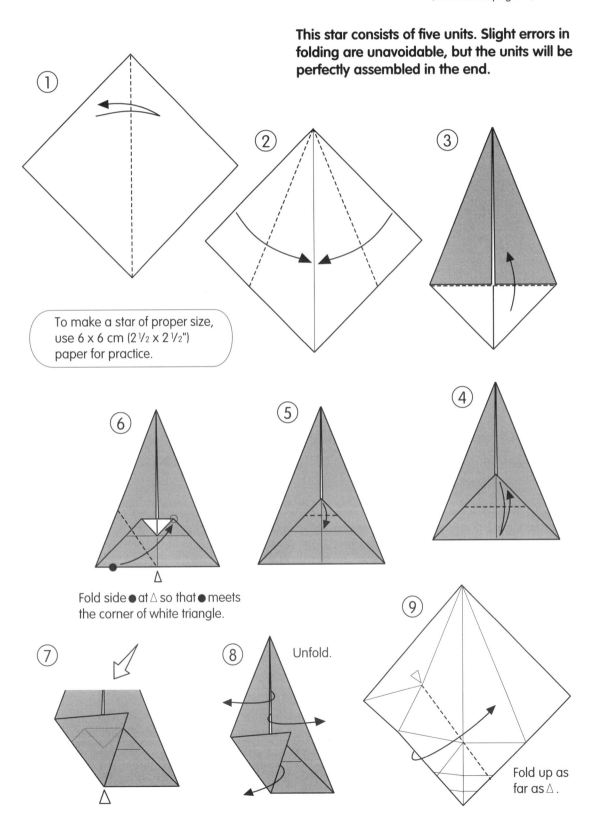

To make a star of proper size, use 6 x 6 cm (2 ½ x 2 ½") paper for practice.

Fold side ● at △ so that ● meets the corner of white triangle.

Unfold.

Fold up as far as △.

74

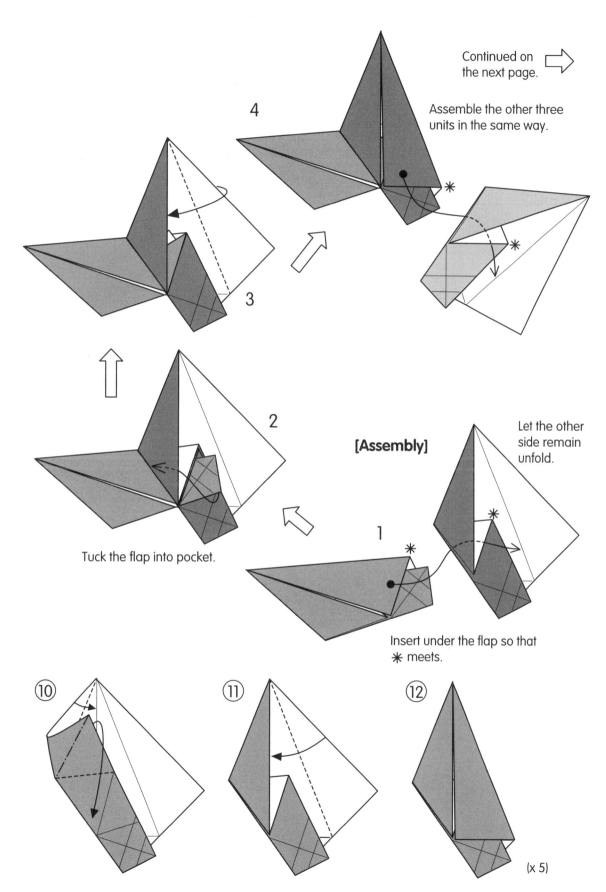

Continued on the next page.

Assemble the other three units in the same way.

4

3

2

[Assembly]

Let the other side remain unfold.

Tuck the flap into pocket.

1

Insert under the flap so that ✳ meets.

⑩

⑪

⑫

(x 5)

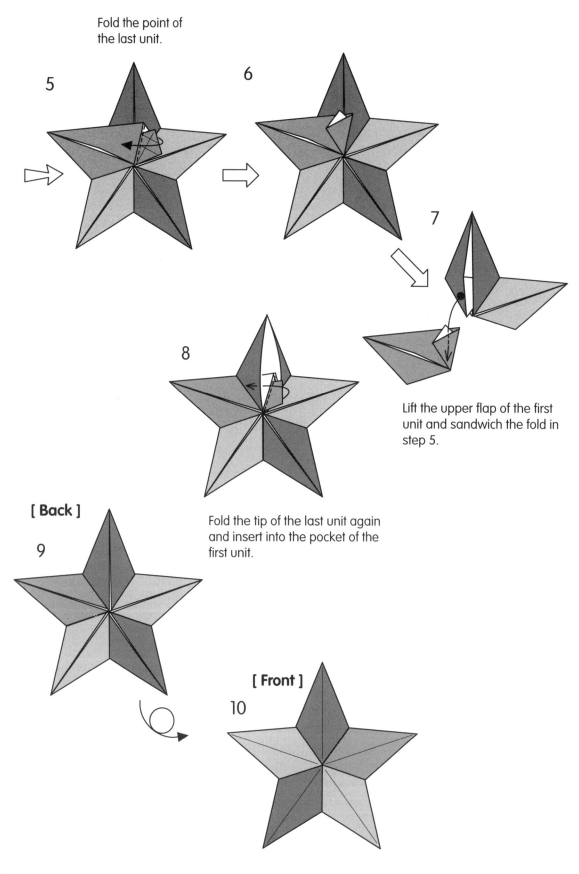

Fold the point of
the last unit.

5

6

7

Lift the upper flap of the first
unit and sandwich the fold in
step 5.

8

[Back]

9

Fold the tip of the last unit again
and insert into the pocket of the
first unit.

[Front]

10

How to fix the last unit

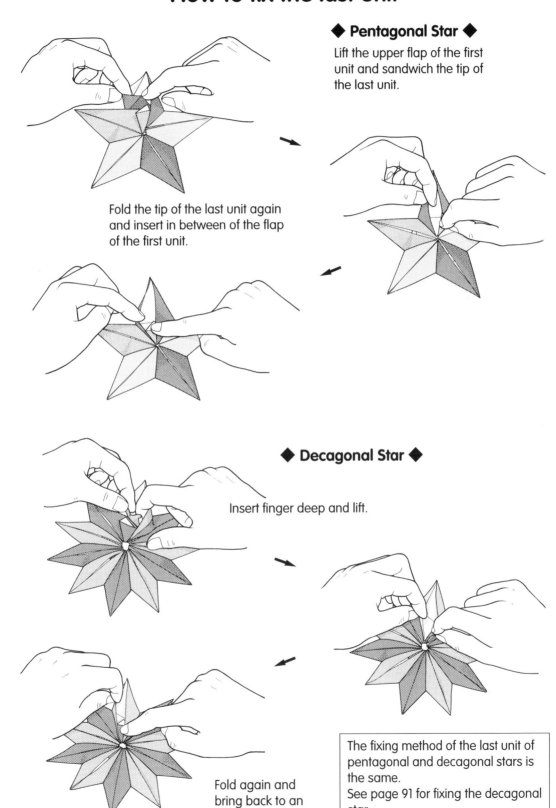

◆ Pentagonal Star ◆

Lift the upper flap of the first unit and sandwich the tip of the last unit.

Fold the tip of the last unit again and insert in between of the flap of the first unit.

◆ Decagonal Star ◆

Insert finger deep and lift.

Fold again and bring back to an original form.

The fixing method of the last unit of pentagonal and decagonal stars is the same.
See page 91 for fixing the decagonal star.

Accessory Part 1

(Pictured on page 15)

Insert various parts in pentagonal and decagonal stars. They look gorgeous like fireworks and flowers.

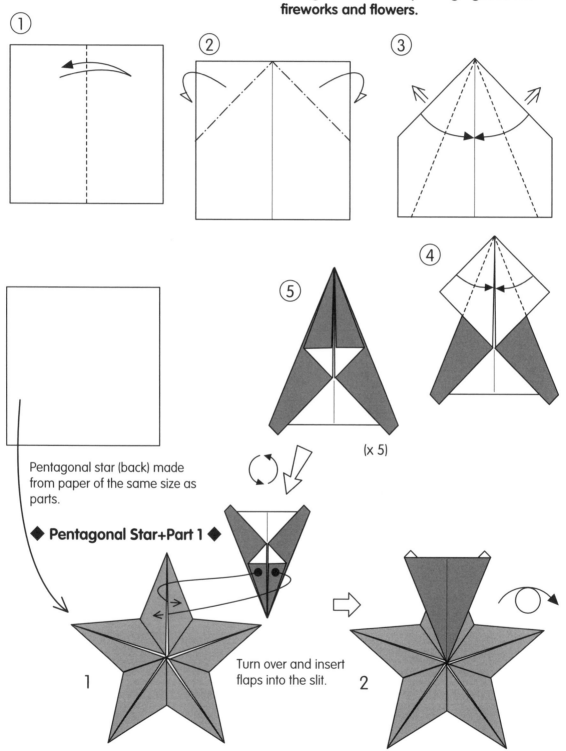

Pentagonal star (back) made from paper of the same size as parts.

(x 5)

◆ **Pentagonal Star+Part 1** ◆

1

Turn over and insert flaps into the slit.

2

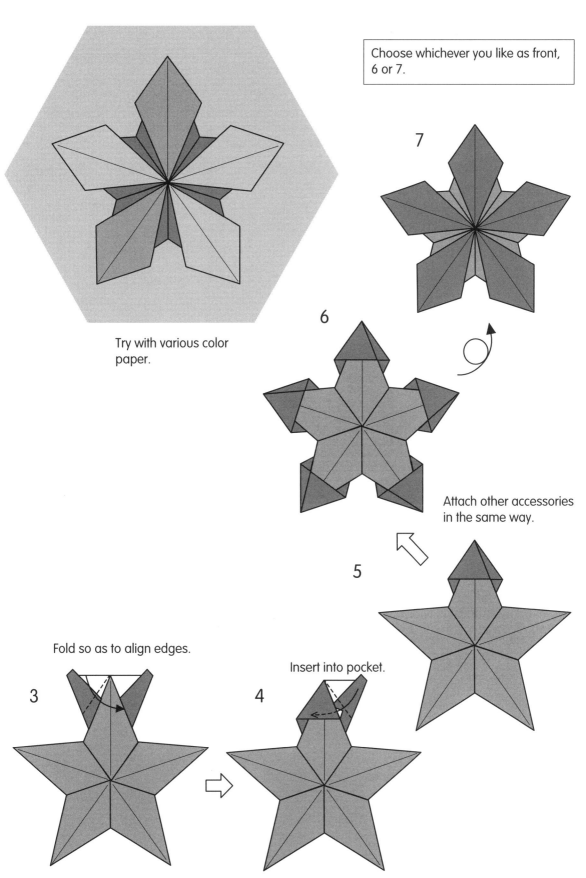

Try with various color paper.

Choose whichever you like as front, 6 or 7.

7

6

Attach other accessories in the same way.

5

Fold so as to align edges.

3

Insert into pocket.

4

79

Accessory Part 2

(Pictured on page 15)

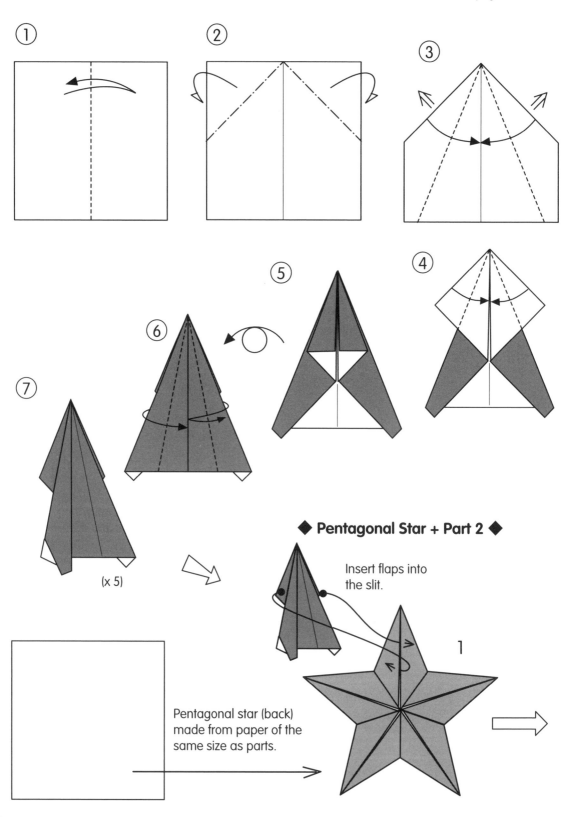

◆ **Pentagonal Star + Part 2** ◆

Insert flaps into the slit.

Pentagonal star (back) made from paper of the same size as parts.

(x 5)

1

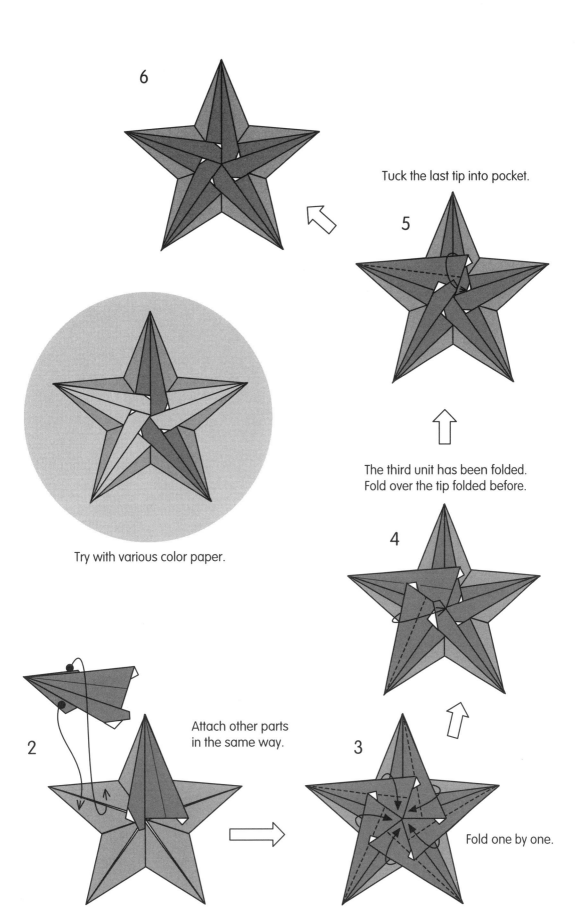

6

Tuck the last tip into pocket.

5

Try with various color paper.

The third unit has been folded.
Fold over the tip folded before.

4

Attach other parts
in the same way.

2

3

Fold one by one.

81

Accessory Part 3

(Pictured on page 15)

If you get precise measurements of parts as shown below, you can make a firm and solid star. If you use paper of ¼, it easily comes off, so a dab of glue on necessary parts will ensure firm assembly.

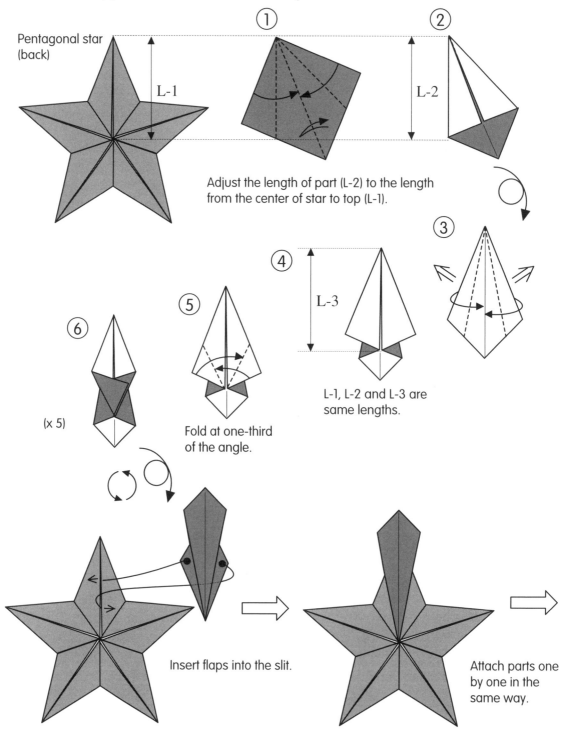

Pentagonal star (back)

L-1

① ②

L-2

Adjust the length of part (L-2) to the length from the center of star to top (L-1).

③

④

L-3

⑤

⑥

(x 5)

L-1, L-2 and L-3 are same lengths.

Fold at one-third of the angle.

Insert flaps into the slit.

Attach parts one by one in the same way.

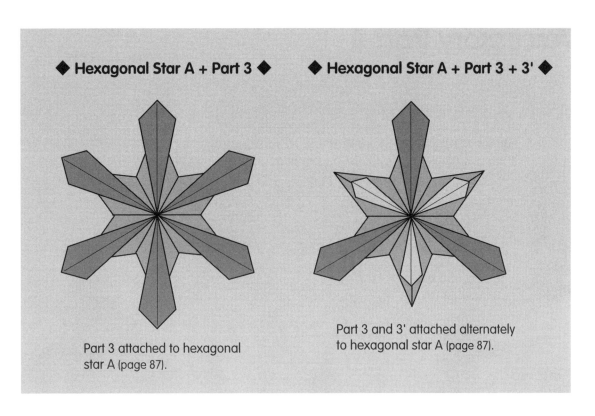

◆ Hexagonal Star A + Part 3 ◆

Part 3 attached to hexagonal star A (page 87).

◆ Hexagonal Star A + Part 3 + 3' ◆

Part 3 and 3' attached alternately to hexagonal star A (page 87).

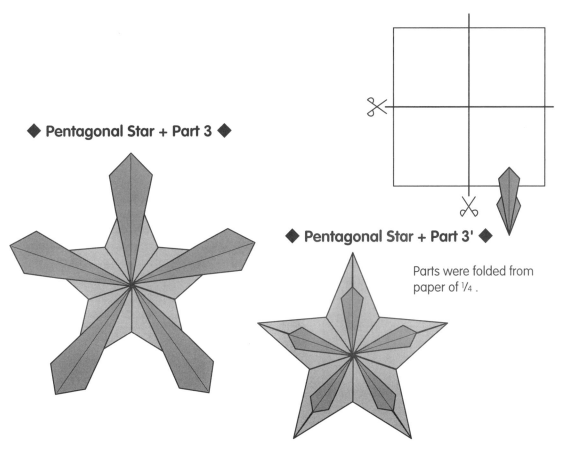

◆ Pentagonal Star + Part 3 ◆

◆ Pentagonal Star + Part 3' ◆

Parts were folded from paper of ¼ .

83

Accessory Part 4

(Pictured on page 15)

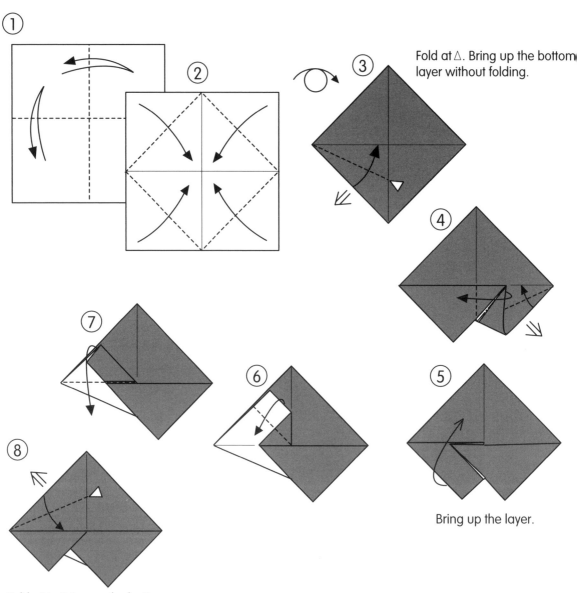

Fold at △. Bring up the bottom layer without folding.

Bring up the layer.

Fold at △. Bring up the bottom layer without folding.

Bring down the layer.

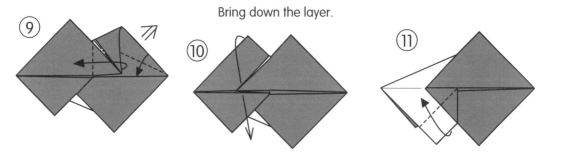

84

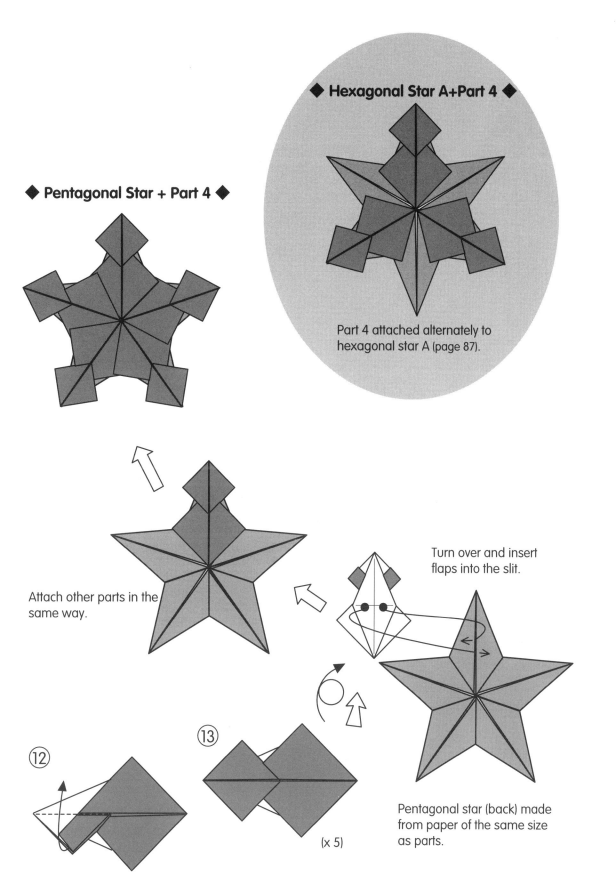

◆ Hexagonal Star A+Part 4 ◆

Part 4 attached alternately to hexagonal star A (page 87).

◆ Pentagonal Star + Part 4 ◆

Attach other parts in the same way.

Turn over and insert flaps into the slit.

⑫

⑬

(× 5)

Pentagonal star (back) made from paper of the same size as parts.

85

Hexagonal Star A

(Pictured on pages 15~16)

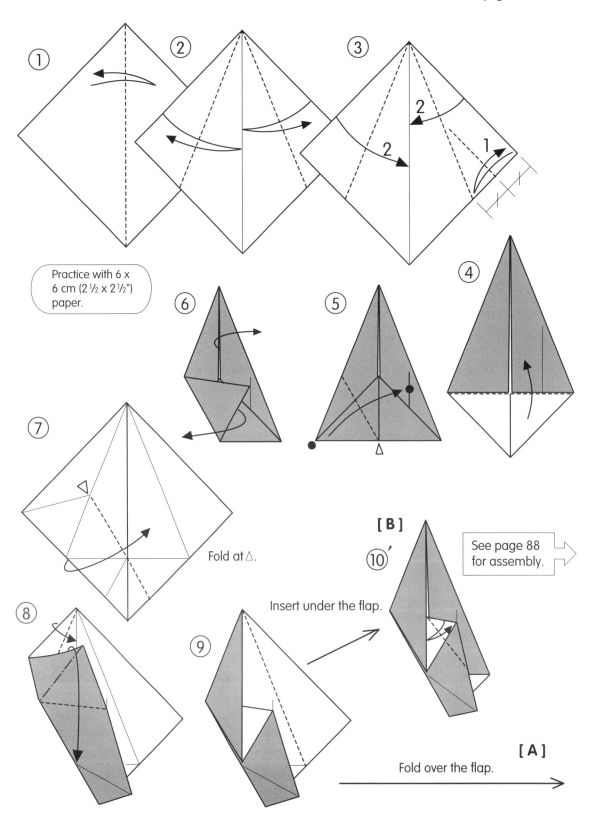

①

②

③

2

2

1

Practice with 6 x 6 cm (2 ½ x 2 ½") paper.

④

⑤

⑥

⑦

Fold at △.

⑧

⑨

⑩′

[B]

Insert under the flap.

See page 88 for assembly.

[A]

Fold over the flap.

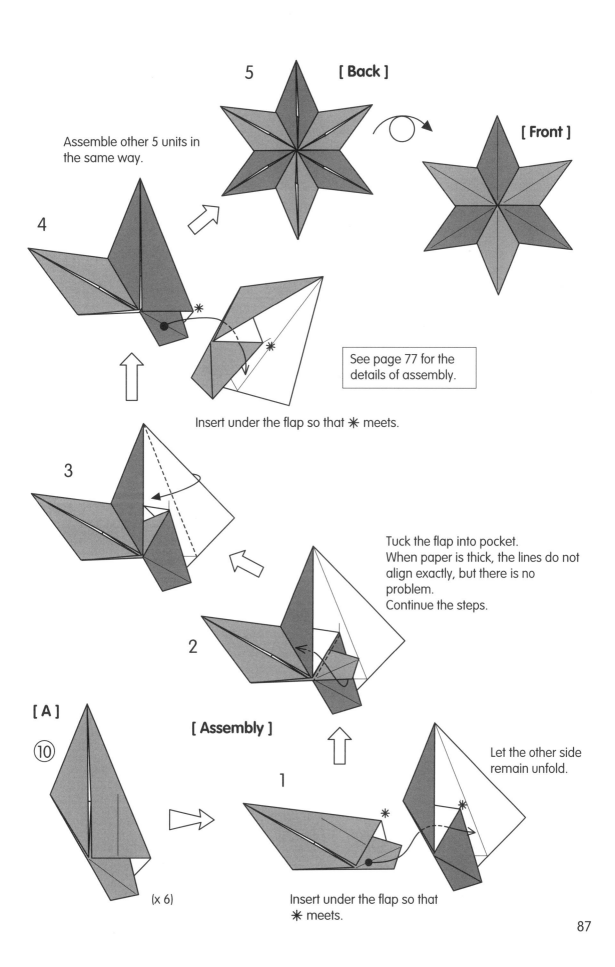

5

[Back]

Assemble other 5 units in the same way.

[Front]

4

See page 77 for the details of assembly.

Insert under the flap so that ✳ meets.

3

Tuck the flap into pocket.
When paper is thick, the lines do not align exactly, but there is no problem.
Continue the steps.

2

[A]

⑩

[Assembly]

1

Let the other side remain unfold.

(x 6)

Insert under the flap so that ✳ meets.

Hexagonal Star B

(Pictured on page 16)

Begin with B ⑩′ on page 86.

[Assembly]

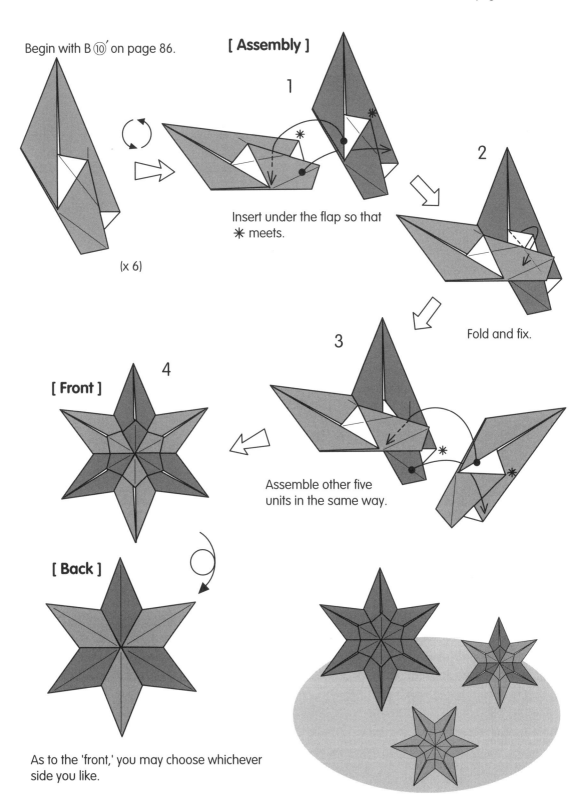

1

Insert under the flap so that
✳ meets.

2

Fold and fix.

3

Assemble other five
units in the same way.

4

[Front]

[Back]

As to the 'front,' you may choose whichever
side you like.

(x 6)

[Measurement of Parts]

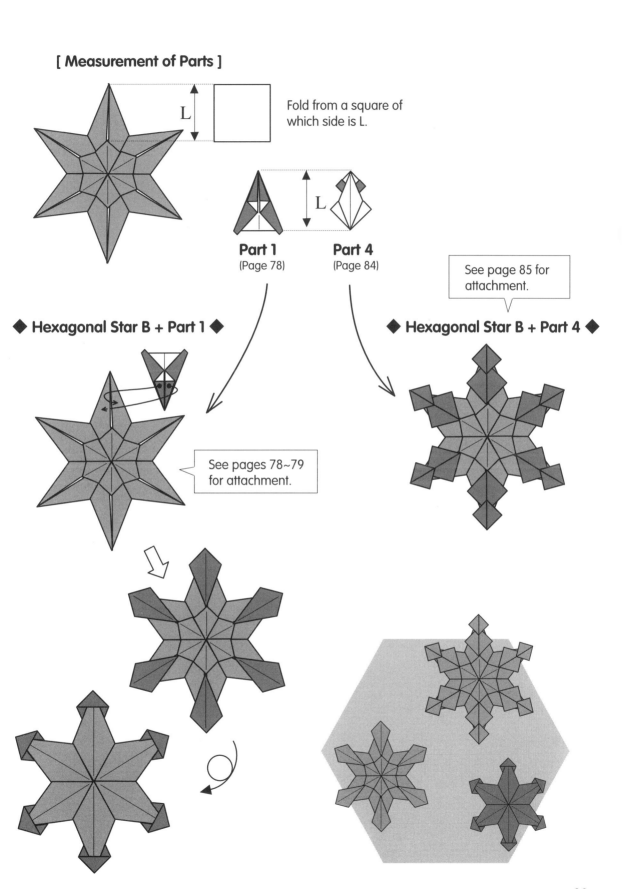

L

Fold from a square of
which side is L.

L

Part 1
(Page 78)

Part 4
(Page 84)

See page 85 for
attachment.

◆ **Hexagonal Star B + Part 1** ◆

◆ **Hexagonal Star B + Part 4** ◆

See pages 78~79
for attachment.

Decagonal Star A

(Pictured on page 15)

Slight errors in folding are unavoidable, but they are no problem when completed.

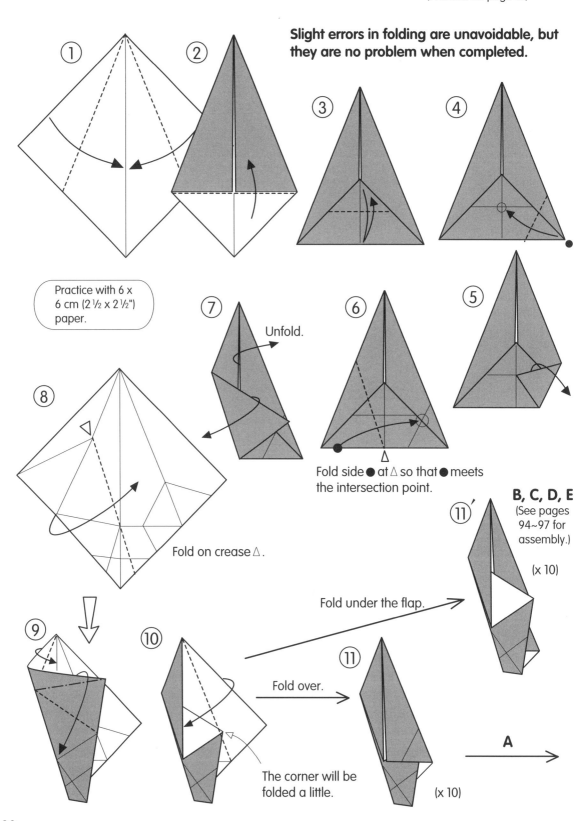

Practice with 6 x 6 cm (2 ½ x 2 ½") paper.

Unfold.

Fold on crease △.

Fold side ● at △ so that ● meets the intersection point.

Fold under the flap.

Fold over.

The corner will be folded a little.

B, C, D, E (See pages 94~97 for assembly.)

(x 10)

(x 10)

A

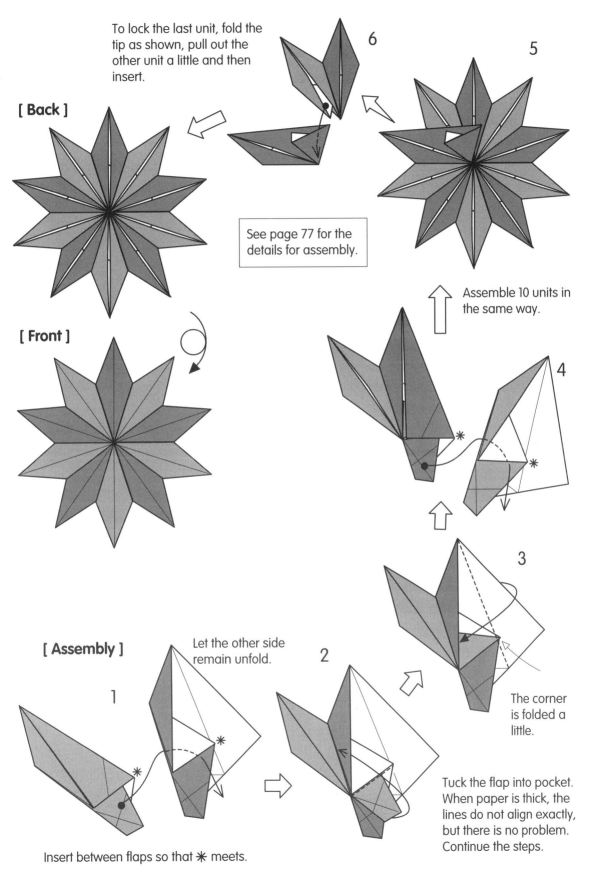

To lock the last unit, fold the tip as shown, pull out the other unit a little and then insert.

6

5

[Back]

See page 77 for the details for assembly.

Assemble 10 units in the same way.

[Front]

4

3

The corner is folded a little.

[Assembly]

Let the other side remain unfold.

2

1

Tuck the flap into pocket. When paper is thick, the lines do not align exactly, but there is no problem. Continue the steps.

Insert between flaps so that ✳ meets.

[Measurement of Decagonal Star and Parts] (Pictured on page 15)

Let's attach parts to decagonal star A. If the occasion requires, fold any corner of the unit to lock it perfectly.

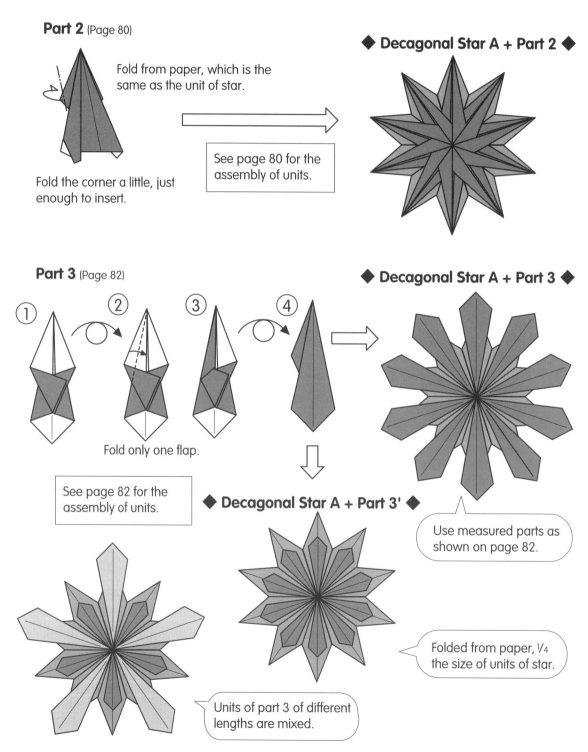

Part 2 (Page 80)

Fold from paper, which is the same as the unit of star.

Fold the corner a little, just enough to insert.

See page 80 for the assembly of units.

◆ **Decagonal Star A + Part 2** ◆

Part 3 (Page 82)

① ② ③ ④

Fold only one flap.

See page 82 for the assembly of units.

◆ **Decagonal Star A + Part 3** ◆

◆ **Decagonal Star A + Part 3'** ◆

Use measured parts as shown on page 82.

Folded from paper, ¼ the size of units of star.

Units of part 3 of different lengths are mixed.

Part 4 (Page 84)

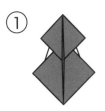

① From paper, which is
the same size as the
units of star.

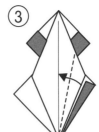

② Fold only one flap to
insert into the slit.

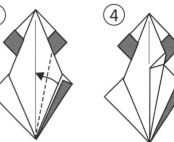

③

④

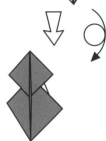

◆ Basic Decagonal Star + Part 4 ◆

See page 85 for the
assembly of units.

Units of different color are used.

Units are attached alternately.

Decagonal Star B

(Pictured on page 14)

Begin with step ⑪' on page 90.

It becomes 'B' or 'C', depending on the final method of locking.

[Assembly]

1

2

Fold back and lock it.

(x 10)

Insert between flaps so that ✳ meets.

3

L

L is a yardstick by which parts are attached.

Assemble 10 units in the same way.

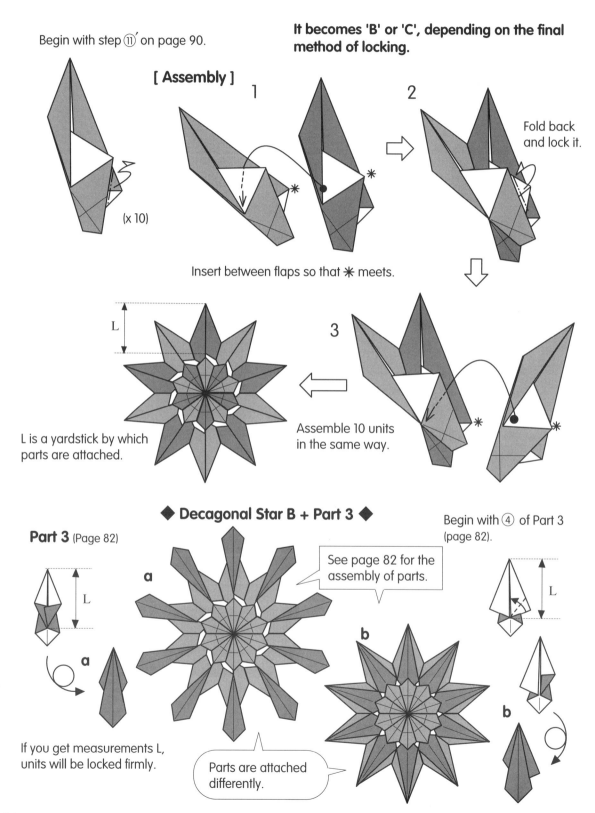

◆ **Decagonal Star B + Part 3** ◆

Part 3 (Page 82)

Begin with ④ of Part 3 (page 82).

L

a

See page 82 for the assembly of parts.

a

b

b

L

If you get measurements L, units will be locked firmly.

Parts are attached differently.

94

Decagonal Star C

(Pictured on page 15)

Begin with step ⑪´
on page 90.

[Assembly]

1

(x 10)

Insert between flaps so that ✳ meets.

2

Assemble 10 units in
the same way.

3

5

4

Tuck in here.

Tuck 10 corners in and
lock all.

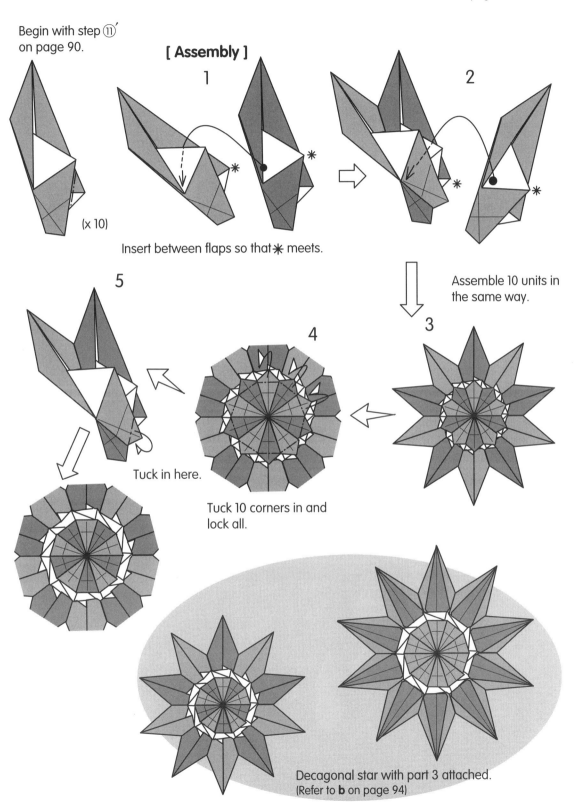

Decagonal star with part 3 attached.
(Refer to **b** on page 94)

Decagonal Star D

(Pictured on page 10)

**It becomes 'D' or 'E', depending on the final method of locking.
Parts may also be attached.**

Begin with step ⑪' on page 90.

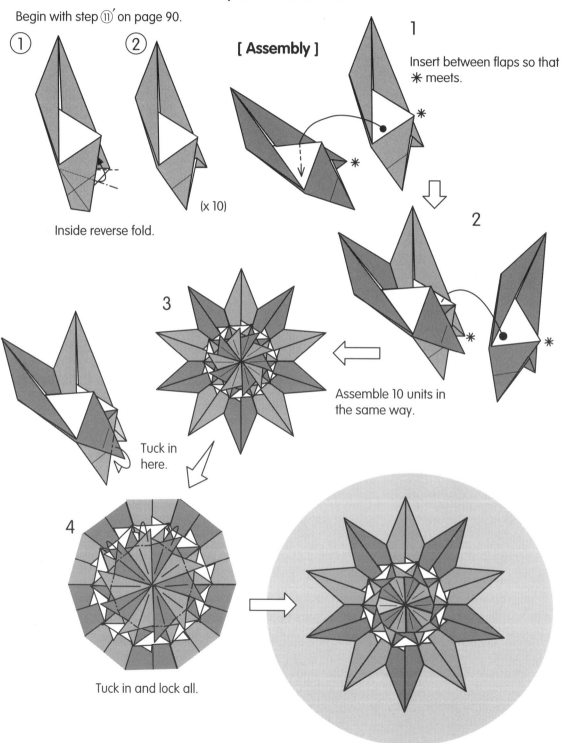

① ②

[Assembly]

1

Insert between flaps so that
✳ meets.

(x 10)

Inside reverse fold.

2

Assemble 10 units in
the same way.

3

Tuck in
here.

4

Tuck in and lock all.

96

Decagonal Star E

(Pictured on pages 14~15)

Begin with step ⑪′ on page 90.

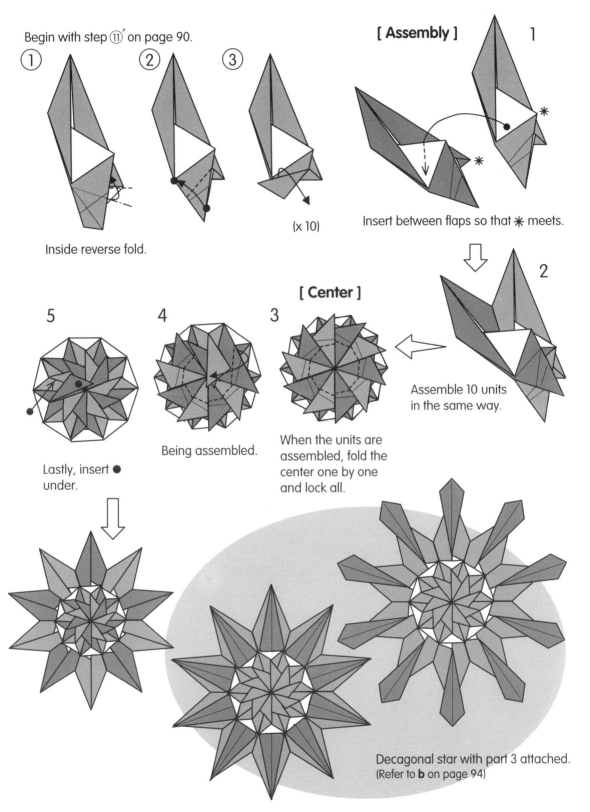

① ② ③

Inside reverse fold.

(x 10)

[Assembly] 1

Insert between flaps so that ✳ meets.

2

Assemble 10 units in the same way.

[Center]

3

When the units are assembled, fold the center one by one and lock all.

4

Being assembled.

5

Lastly, insert ● under.

Decagonal star with part 3 attached.
(Refer to **b** on page 94)

If you have time to spare

'Since I have retired, I have now enough time to enjoy origami at last.' I often receive such letters. In reply, I say, 'That's fine. I hope you make a good start.' 'Since I have to prepare for an entrance examination, I have no time to enjoy origami.' Sometimes I receive such letters. In reply, I say, 'It is a great asset that you have once been immersed in origami in your childhood. Sometime In your future life, the time will surely come when you can revive your origami.' My replies may sound like a counselor's advice, but I really meant what I said.

Most children love origami. They are absorbed in folding paper. They joyfully say, 'I've made it' and show the work to everyone around them. The word implies that they have made the work by their own hands and, at the same time, it shows a wonder that such an interesting thing has been produced. Among hobbies, there are few that both adults and children can enjoy with wonder on an equal footing.

If there is something urgent on you mind, you will be unable to devote yourself to origami. When it is off your mind, get to work on origami. Many people take up origami to forget what is on their mind and worries, and then they can pick themselves up again. You are busy, but if you find time to spare, try origami.

By the way, how about those who are absorbed in origami and have no time?

Chapter 4

Packages

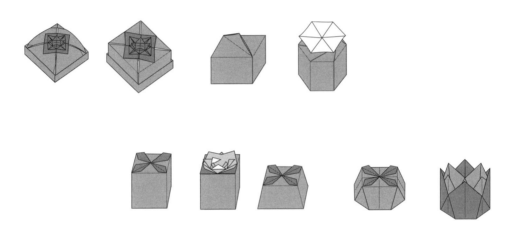

For Practical Use and Play
--------- Enjoy folding

The containers introduced in this chapter will be about the size of your palm. Since they are folded, thick paper is not suitable. It is possible to make larger containers, but they are something out of tune. Containers of origami are not strong and they can hold only light things. Accordingly, gentle handling is important.

They are intended for play rather than for practical use. They are heartwarming. That will be because the folder's intent is conveyed to the receiver.

Cake Box 1 A lid of flower

(Pictured on page 17)

The square body is covered with a dome-like lid.
The lid is locked with a flower so as not to come
apart.

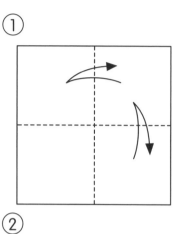

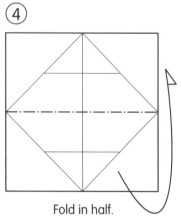

Fold in half.

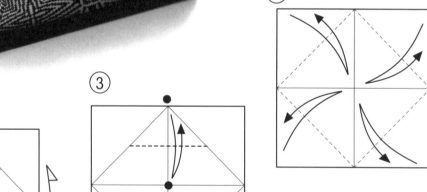

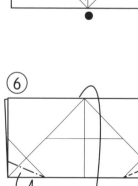

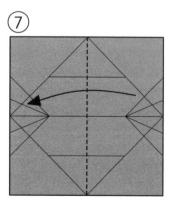

Make creases and unfold.

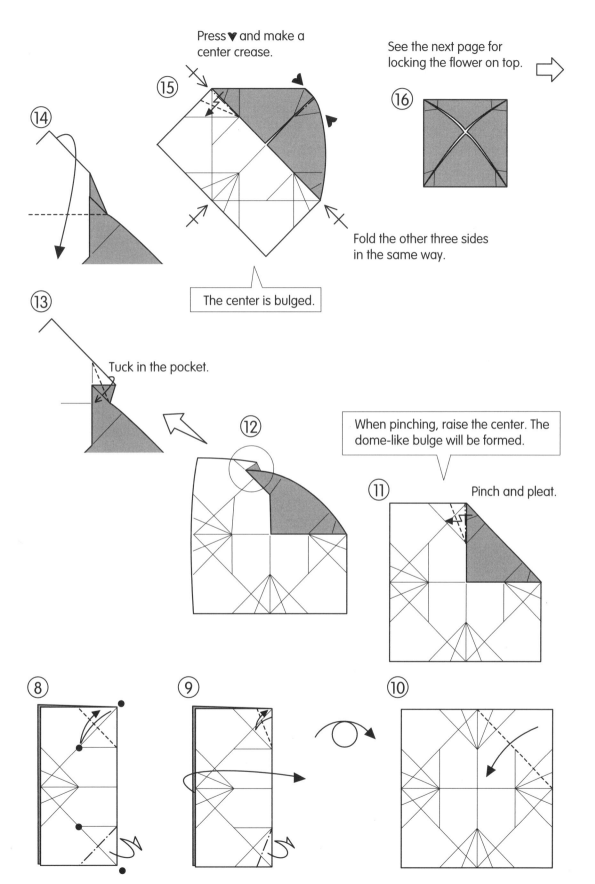

Press ▼ and make a center crease.

⑮

⑭

⑬

Tuck in the pocket.

The center is bulged.

⑯

See the next page for locking the flower on top. ⇨

Fold the other three sides in the same way.

⑫

When pinching, raise the center. The dome-like bulge will be formed.

⑪

Pinch and pleat.

⑧

⑨

⑩

◆ Knob of flower ◆

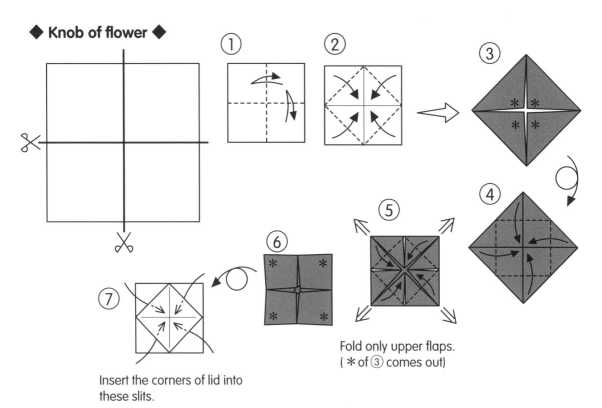

① ② ③

④

⑤

Fold only upper flaps.
(✳ of ③ comes out)

⑥

⑦

Insert the corners of lid into
these slits.

[Assembly]

[View from top]

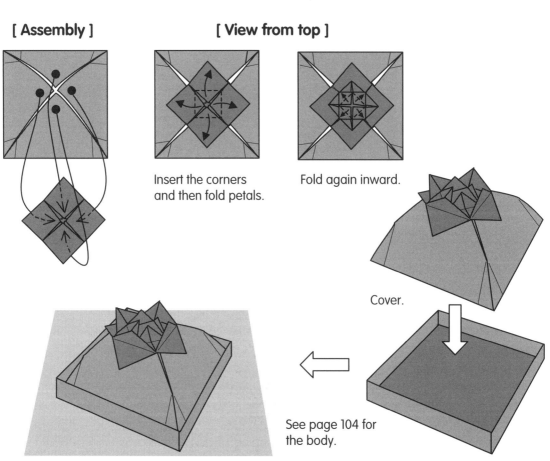

Insert the corners
and then fold petals.

Fold again inward.

Cover.

See page 104 for
the body.

Cake Box 1 Plain lid

(Pictured on page 17)

If you turn over 'flower,' you can get a plain lid.

Begin with ⑪ on page 101.

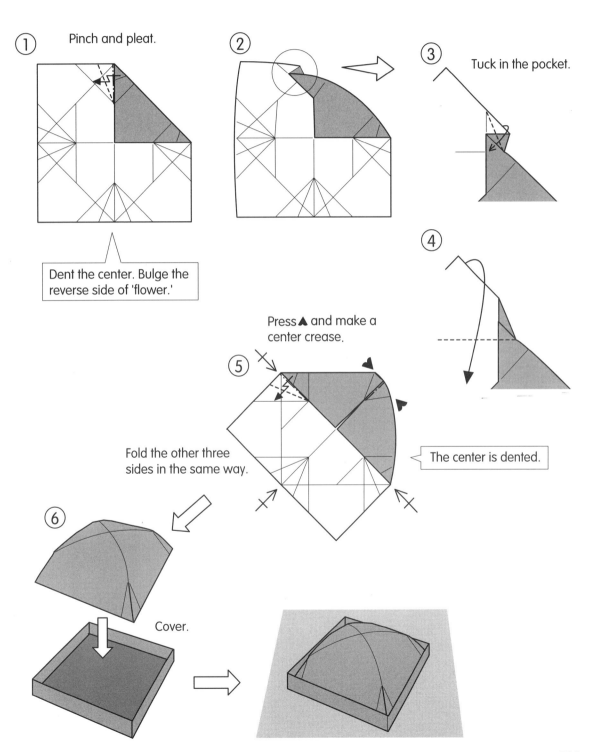

① Pinch and pleat.

Dent the center. Bulge the reverse side of 'flower.'

②

③ Tuck in the pocket.

④

Press ▲ and make a center crease.

⑤

The center is dented.

Fold the other three sides in the same way.

⑥

Cover.

103

Cake Box 1 Body

(Pictured on page 17)

Application of traditional 'masu' (measure). The depth depends on the width of ④.

①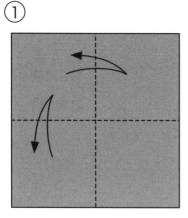

②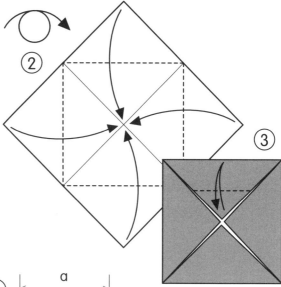

③

Fold only the upper layer.

Make creases and unfold.

⑤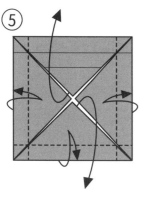

④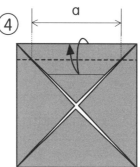

The width of (a) is the side of the box. If you change the width, you can make nesting boxing.

⑥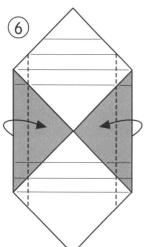

⑦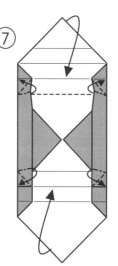

⑧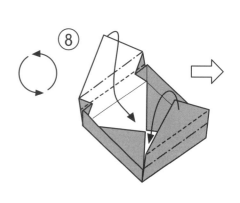

◆ Bottom 1 ◆

The length of the side of the square is twice as large as (a).

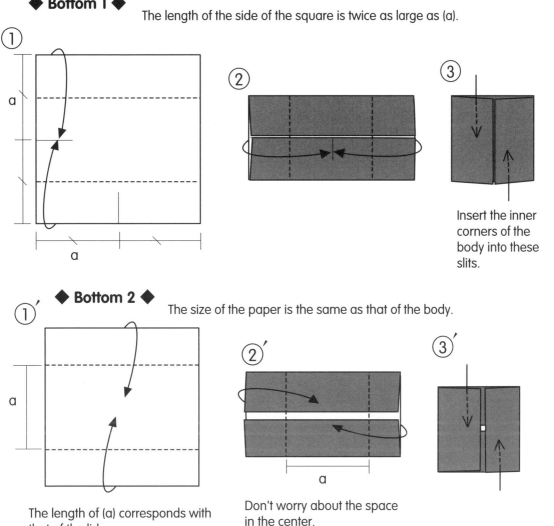

Insert the inner corners of the body into these slits.

◆ Bottom 2 ◆

The size of the paper is the same as that of the body.

The length of (a) corresponds with that of the lid.
You had better fold the bottom a little smaller than the body.

Don't worry about the space in the center.

[Assembly]

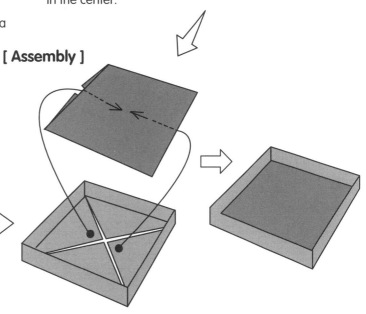

Cake Box 2

(Pictured on page 17)

Turn the traditional 'masu' (measure) inside out and make it the lid. Attach a knob of flower on top.

◆ Lid ◆

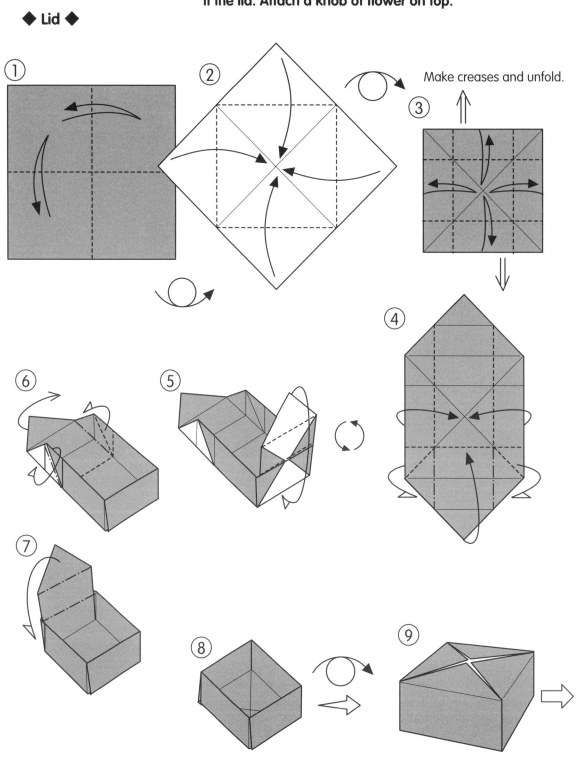

Make creases and unfold.

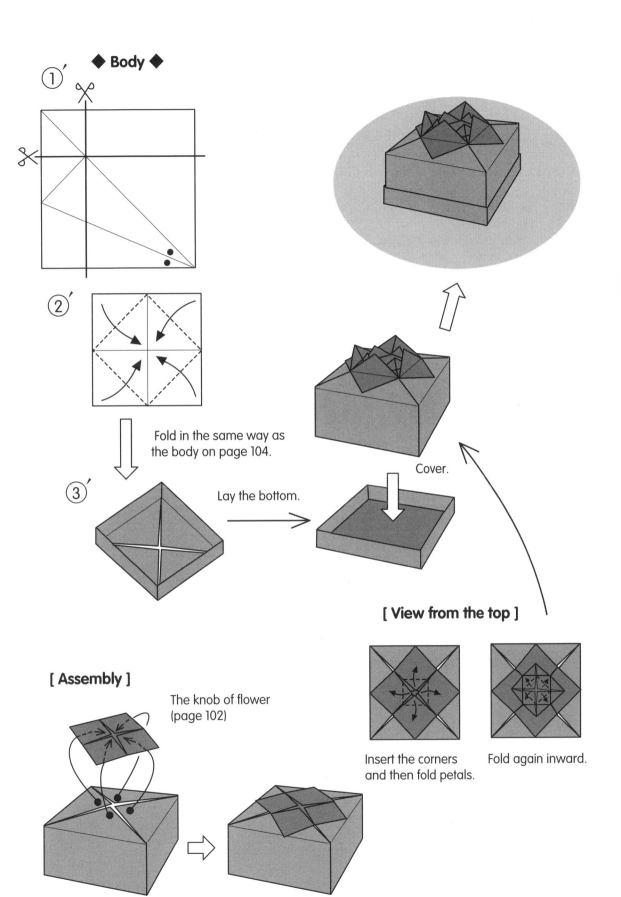

◆ Body ◆

①′

②′

Fold in the same way as the body on page 104.

③′

Lay the bottom.

Cover.

[View from the top]

Insert the corners and then fold petals.

Fold again inward.

[Assembly]

The knob of flower (page 102)

107

Square Package

(Pictured on page 19)

Use 21 x 30 cm (8 ½ x 12 ") paper for practice.

A cylindrical package with four sides made from a piece of paper. It is good for present and putting a potpourri in it. If you use a little thicker paper, you can make a nice and sturdy package.

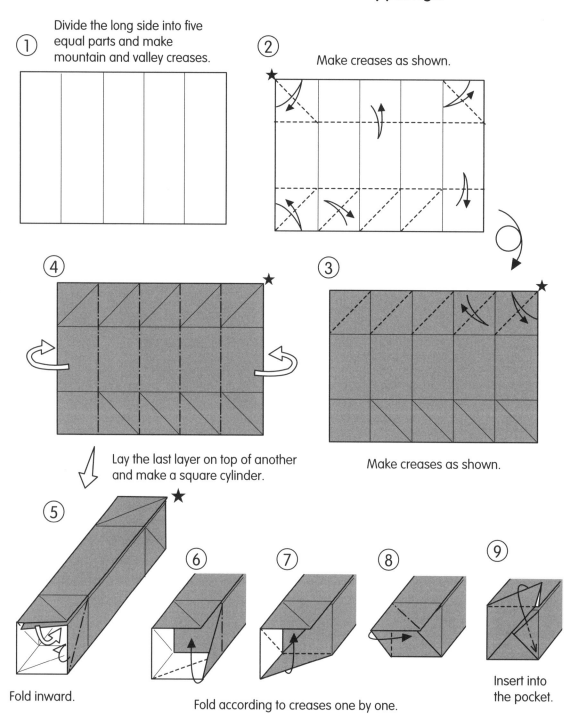

① Divide the long side into five equal parts and make mountain and valley creases.

② Make creases as shown.

③ Make creases as shown.

④ Lay the last layer on top of another and make a square cylinder.

⑤ Fold inward.

⑥ ⑦ Fold according to creases one by one.

⑧

⑨ Insert into the pocket.

108

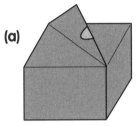

(a)

You can seal the flaps with glue.

⬆

You may let the top as it is.

⑫´

(b)

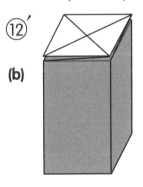

⑬

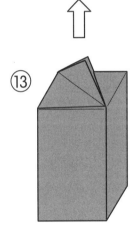

⬆

Put something in and then twist and flatten the top.

Lift the flaps.

⑩ ⑪ ⑫

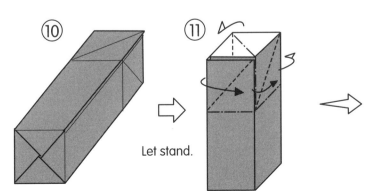

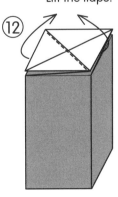

Let stand.

Package with Six Sides · A

(Pictured on page 19)

Use 21 x 30 cm (8 ½ x 12 ") paper for practice.

This package has six sides. The point is how to fold the bottom. If you use a little thicker paper, you can make a sturdy package, though it depends on the size.

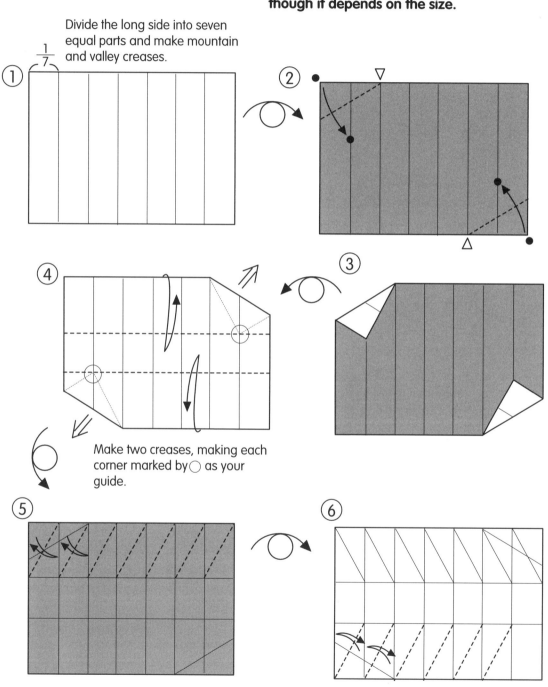

Divide the long side into seven equal parts and make mountain and valley creases.

Make two creases, making each corner marked by ◯ as your guide.

Make creases as shown.

Make creases as shown.

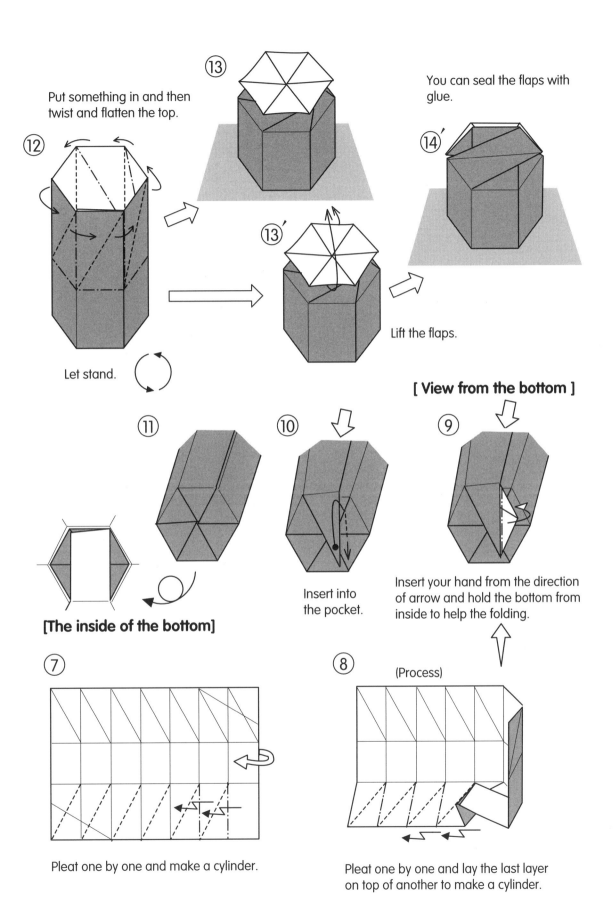

⑬ Put something in and then twist and flatten the top.

⑫ Let stand.

You can seal the flaps with glue.

⑭′

⑬′ Lift the flaps.

[View from the bottom]

⑪

⑩ Insert into the pocket.

⑨ Insert your hand from the direction of arrow and hold the bottom from inside to help the folding.

[The inside of the bottom]

⑦ Pleat one by one and make a cylinder.

⑧ (Process)

Pleat one by one and lay the last layer on top of another to make a cylinder.

Package with Six Sides · B

(Pictured on page 19)

A variation of Package with Six Sides · A

The gray parts show the area that comes into contact with the inside of the outer package.

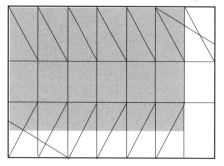

Put thin paper inside.

Fold in the same way as 'A'.

Peel off the thin paper and make it look like a flower.

<Reinforce the package>

Make a cylinder with six sides from thick paper. Fix it into the package and close the top

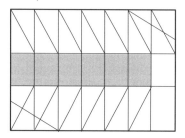

Make about 5 mm (1/8") smaller than the gray parts.

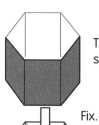

The cylinder with six sides.

Fix.

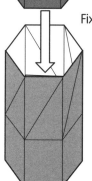

After the cylinder is fixed, close the top.

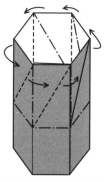

Dice Package

(Pictured on page 20)

Boxes of various shapes are locked with stoppers.

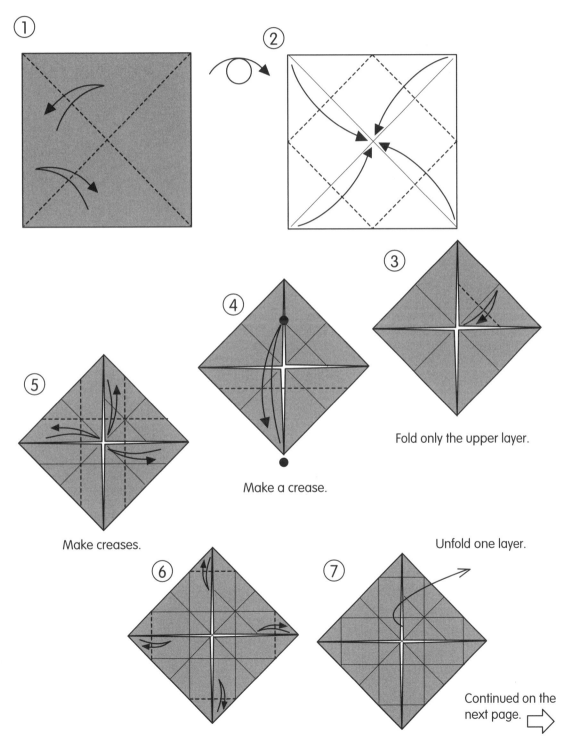

Fold only the upper layer.

Make a crease.

Make creases.

Unfold one layer.

Continued on the
next page. ⇨

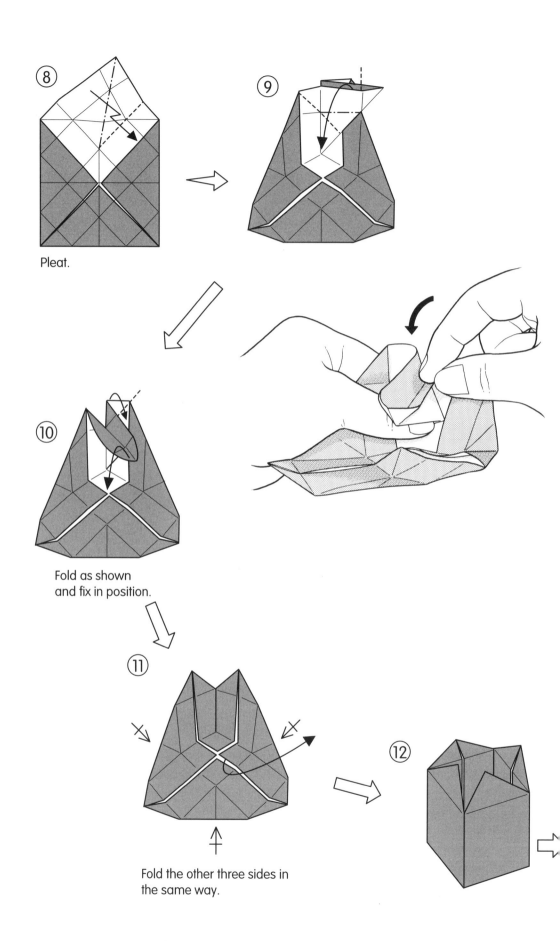

⑧

Pleat.

⑨

⑩

Fold as shown
and fix in position.

⑪

Fold the other three sides in
the same way.

⑫

◆ Stopper 1 ◆

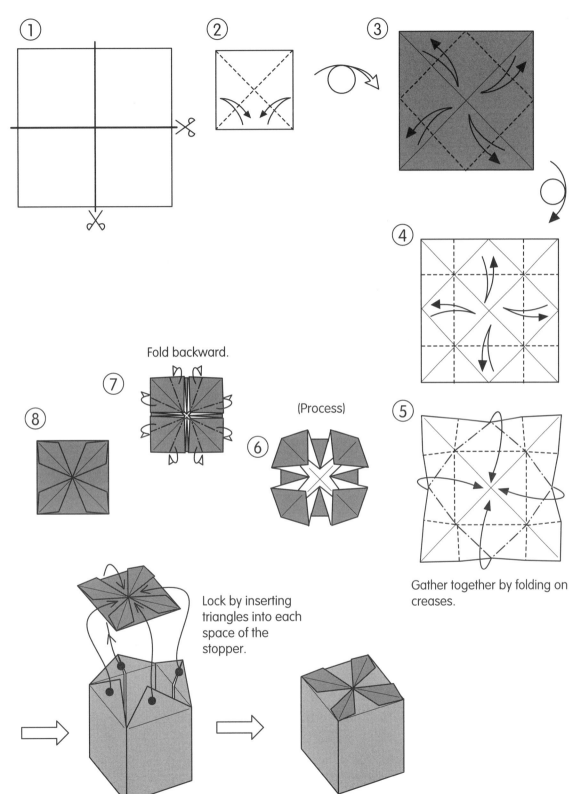

①

②

③

④

⑤
Gather together by folding on creases.

(Process)
⑥

Fold backward.
⑦

⑧

Lock by inserting triangles into each space of the stopper.

◆ Stopper 2 ◆

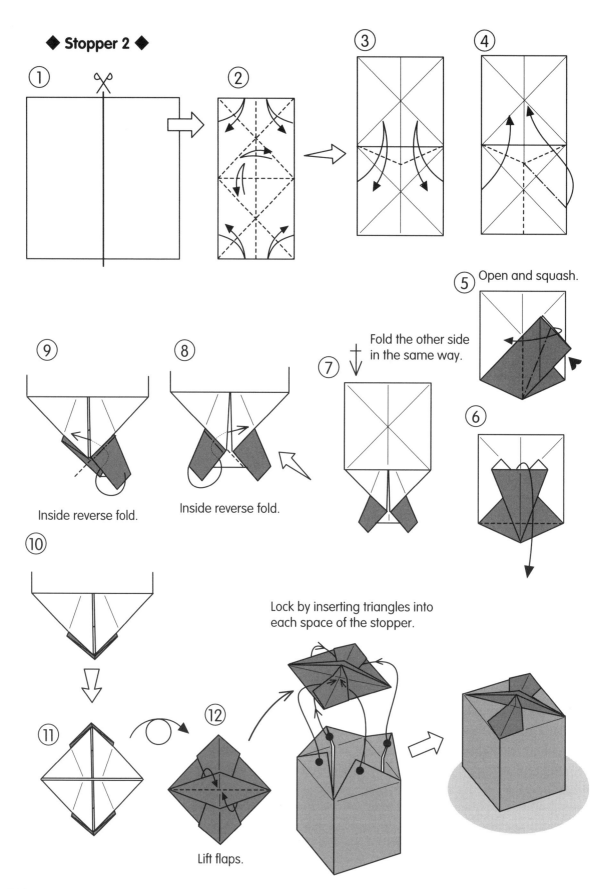

① ②

③ ④

⑤ Open and squash.

⑥

⑦ Fold the other side in the same way.

⑧ Inside reverse fold.

⑨ Inside reverse fold.

⑩

⑪ ⑫ Lift flaps.

Lock by inserting triangles into each space of the stopper.

Picture frame (page 53)

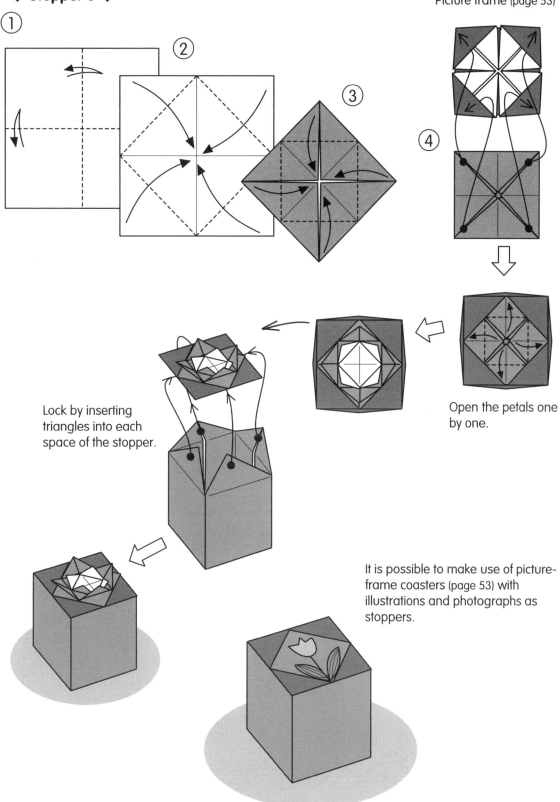

Open the petals one by one.

Lock by inserting triangles into each space of the stopper.

It is possible to make use of picture-frame coasters (page 53) with illustrations and photographs as stoppers.

Half-size Dice Package

(Pictured on page 20)

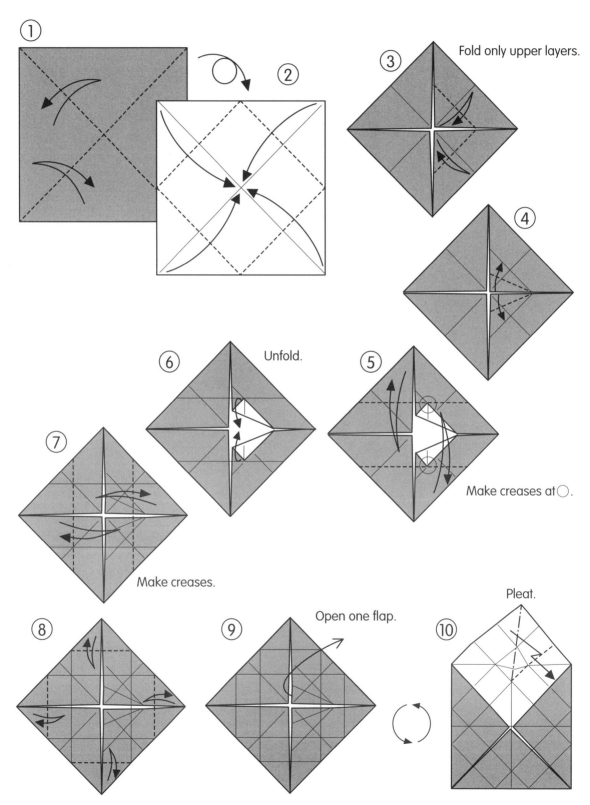

①

②

③ Fold only upper layers.

④

Unfold. ⑥ ⑤

Make creases at ◯.

⑦

Make creases.

⑧ ⑨ Open one flap. ⑩ Pleat.

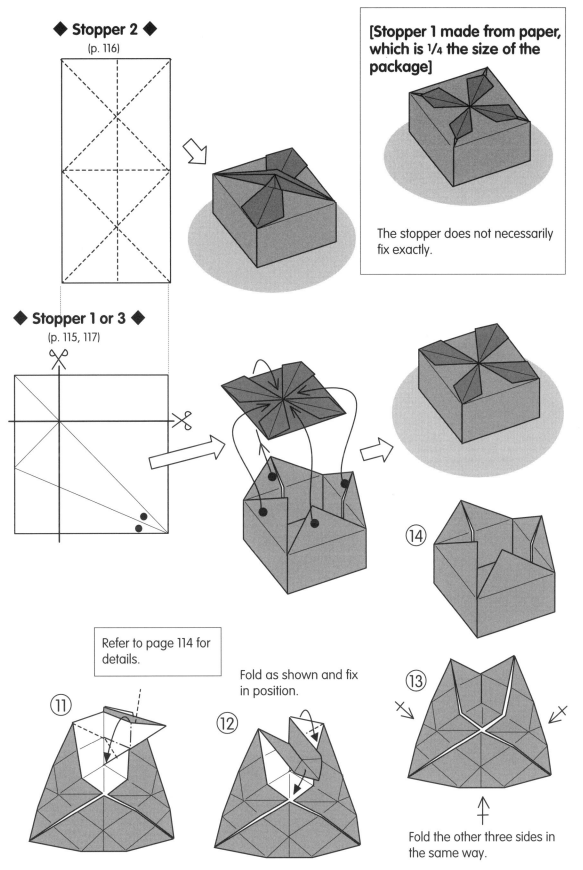

◆ **Stopper 2** ◆
(p. 116)

[Stopper 1 made from paper, which is ¹/₄ the size of the package]

The stopper does not necessarily fix exactly.

◆ **Stopper 1 or 3** ◆
(p. 115, 117)

⑭

Refer to page 114 for details.

⑪

Fold as shown and fix in position.

⑫

⑬

Fold the other three sides in the same way.

119

Trapezoid Package

(Pictured on page 20)

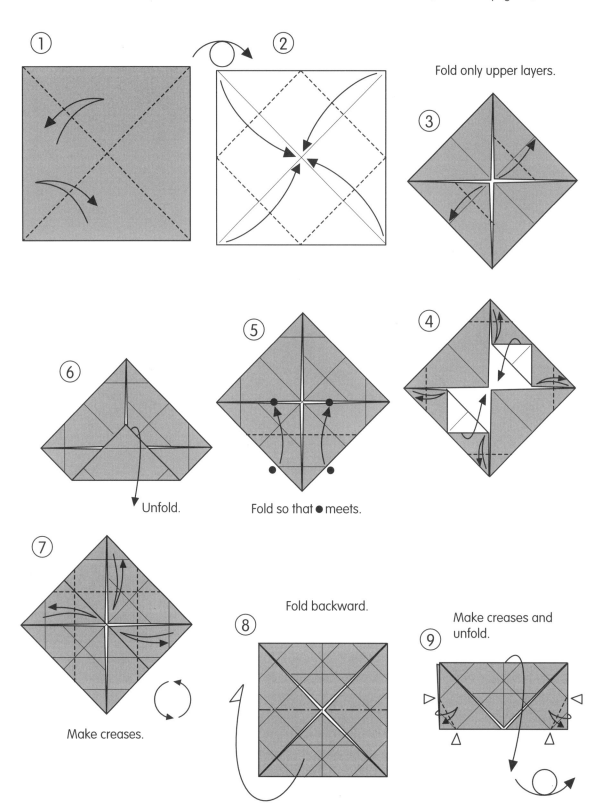

①

②

③ Fold only upper layers.

④

⑤ Fold so that ● meets.

⑥ Unfold.

⑦ Make creases.

⑧ Fold backward.

⑨ Make creases and unfold.

120

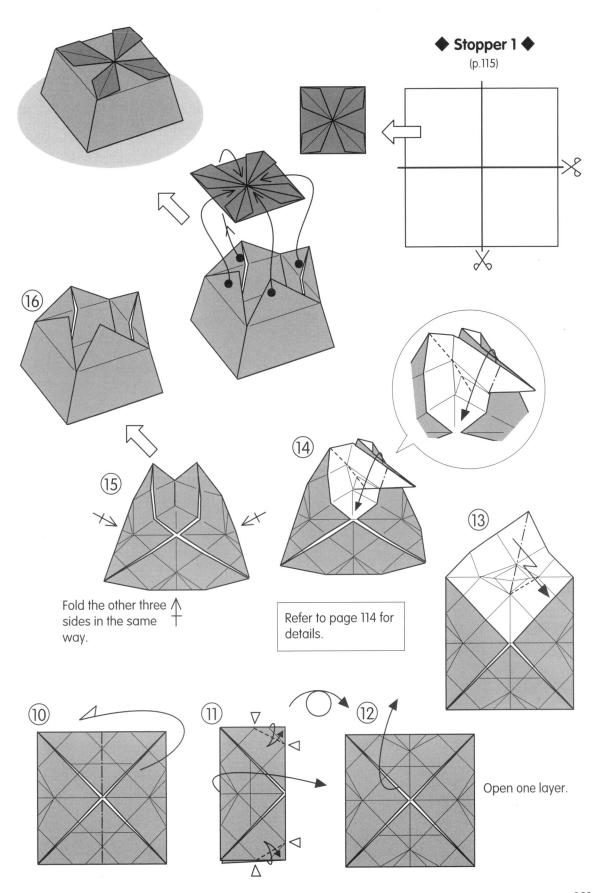

◆ **Stopper 1** ◆
(p.115)

⑯

Fold the other three
sides in the same
way.

Refer to page 114 for
details.

⑮

⑭

⑬

⑩

⑪

⑫

Open one layer.

121

Tulip Cup

(Pictured on page 18)

A container in the shape of a tulip. It can also be used as a package.

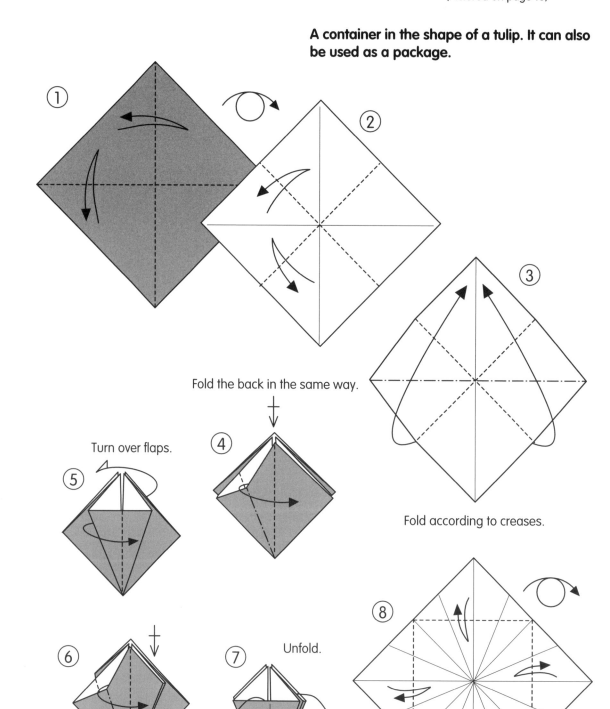

①

②

③

Fold the back in the same way.

④

⑤ Turn over flaps.

Fold according to creases.

⑥

Do the same on the other side.

⑦ Unfold.

⑧

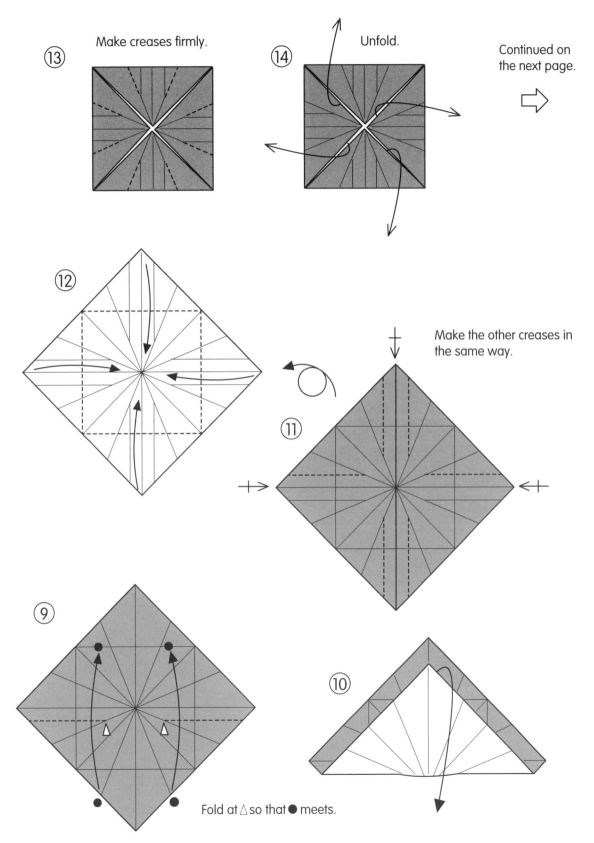

⑬ Make creases firmly.

⑭ Unfold.

Continued on the next page.

⑫

⑪ Make the other creases in the same way.

⑨

⑩

Fold at △ so that ● meets.

123

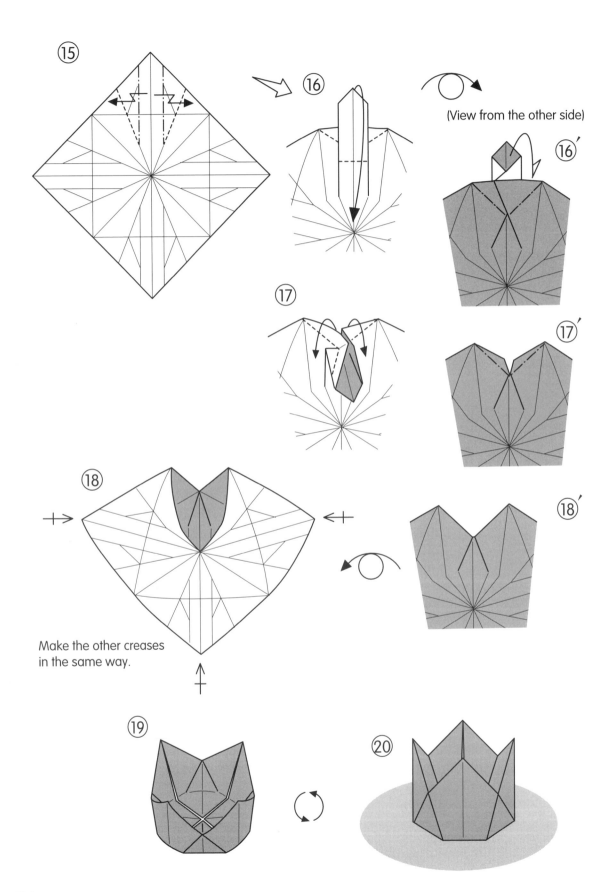

⑮

⑯

(View from the other side)

⑯′

⑰

⑰′

⑱

Make the other creases
in the same way.

⑱′

⑲

⑳

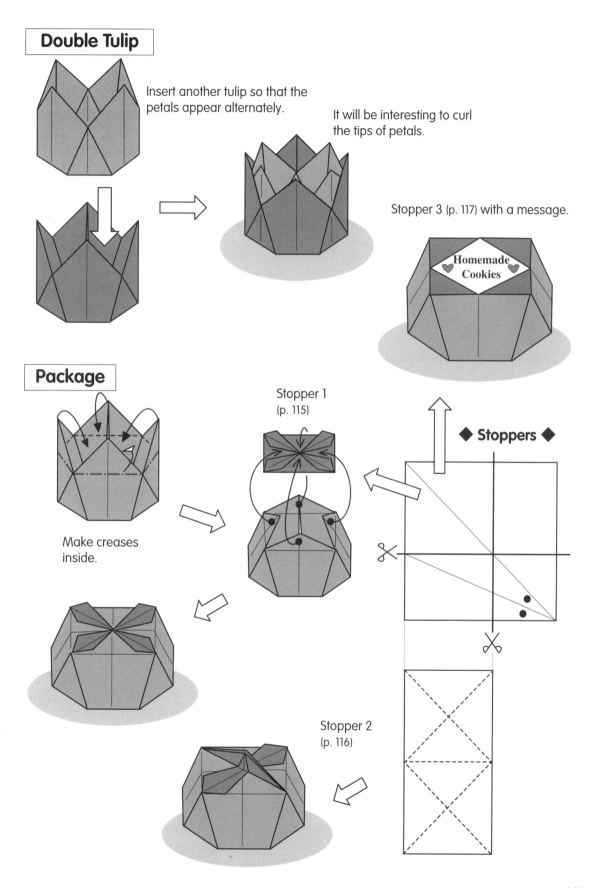

Double Tulip

Insert another tulip so that the petals appear alternately.

It will be interesting to curl the tips of petals.

Stopper 3 (p. 117) with a message.

Homemade Cookies

Package

Make creases inside.

Stopper 1 (p. 115)

Stopper 2 (p. 116)

♦ **Stoppers** ♦

ORIGAMI BOOKS
from Japan Publications

3D ORIGAMI: Step-by-step Illustrations by Yoshie Hatahira et al.
90 pp., 8 1/4 x 10 1/4 in., 24 pp. color, 64 pp. b/w photos and line drawings, paperback.
ISBN: 4-88996-057-0

BRILLIANT ORIGAMI: A Collection of Original Designs by David Brill
240 pp., 7 1/4 x 10 1/4 in., 8 pp. color, 215 pp. line drawings, paperback.
ISBN: 0-87040-896-8

COMPLETE ORIGAMI COLLECTION, THE, by Toshie Takahama
160 pp., 7 1/4 x 10 1/4 in., 8 pp. color, 147 pp. line drawings, paperback.
ISBN: 0-87040-960-3

CREATIVE ORIGAMI by Kunihiko Kasahara
180 pp., 8 1/4 x 11 3/4 in., 8 pp. b/w photos, 160 pp. line drawings, paperback.
ISBN: 0-87040-411-3

FABULOUS ORIGAMI BOXES by Tomoko Fuse
99 pp., 7 1/4 x 10 1/4 in., 18 pp. color, 80 pp. line drawings, paperback.
ISBN: 0-87040-978-6

JOYFUL ORIGAMI BOXES by Tomoko Fuse
96 pp., 7 1/4 x 10 1/4 in., 8 pp. color, 80 pp. line drawings, paperback.
ISBN: 0-87040-974-3

KUSUDAMA: Ball Origami by Makoto Yamaguchi
72 pp., 7 1/4 x 10 1/4 in., 8 pp. color, 65 pp. line drawings, paperback.
ISBN: 4-88996-049-X

MAGIC OF ORIGAMI, THE, by Alice Gray and Kunihiko Kasahara with cooperation
of Lillian Oppenheimer and Origami Center of America
132 pp., 7 1/4 x 10 1/4 in., 122 pp. b/w photos and line drawings, paperback.
ISBN: 0-87040-624-8

ORIGAMI by Hideki Sakata
66 pp., 7 1/4 x 10 1/4 in., 66 pp. full color illustrations, paperback.
ISBN: 0-87040-580-2

ORIGAMI ABC's by Hideki Sakata
48 p., 8 1/4 x 10 1/4 in., 2 color line drawings, paperback.
ISBN: 0-87040-999-9

ORIGAMI ANIMALS by Keiji Kitamura
*88 pp., 8 1/4 x 10 1/4 in., 88 pp. full color illustrations, 12 sheets of origami paper
included, paperback.*
ISBN: 0-87040-941-7

ORIGAMI BOXES by Tomoko Fuse
72 pp., 7 1/4 x 10 1/4 in., 8 pp. color, 60 pp. line drawings, paperback.
ISBN: 0-87040-821-6

ORIGAMI CLASSROOM I by Dokuotei Nakano
*Boxed set, board-book: 24 pp., 6 x 6 in., 24 pp. full color illustrations, plus origami
paper: 6 x 6 in., 54 sheets of rainbow-color paper.*
ISBN: 0-87040-912-3

ORIGAMI CLASSROOM II by Dokuotei Nakano
*Boxed set, board-book: 24 pp., 6 x 6 in., 24 pp. full color illustrations, plus origami
paper: 6 x 6 in., 60 sheets of rainbow-color paper.*
ISBN: 0-87040-938-7

ORIGAMI FOR THE CONNOISSEUR by Kunihiko Kasahara and Toshie Takahama
168 pp., 7 1/4 x 10 1/4 in., 2 color line drawings, paperback.
ISBN: 4-8170-9002-2

PLAYFUL ORIGAMI by Reiko Asou
96 pp., 8 1/4 x 10 1/4 in., 48 pp. full color illustrations, 10 sheets of origami paper included, paperback.
ISBN: 0-87040-827-5

ORIGAMI HEARTS by Francis Ow Mun Yin
120 pp., 7 1/4 x 10 1/4 in., 8 pp. color, 104 pp. line drawings, paperback.
ISBN: 0-87040-957-3

ORIGAMI MADE EASY by Kunihiko Kasahara
128 pp., 6 x 8 1/4 in., 113 pp. b/w photos and line drawings, paperback.
ISBN: 0-87040-253-6

ORIGAMI OMNIBUS: Paper-folding for Everybody by Kunihiko Kasahara
384 pp., 7 1/4 x 10 1/4 in., 8 pp. color, 360 pp. line drawings, paperback.
ISBN: 4-8170-9001-4

ORIGAMI TREASURE CHEST by Keiji Kitamura
80 pp., 8 1/4 x 10 1/4 in., full color, paperback.
ISBN: 0-87040-868-2

PAPER MAGIC: Pop-up Paper Craft by Masahiro Chatani
92 pp., 7 1/4 x 10 1/4 in., 16 pp. color, 72 pp. b/w photos and line drawings, paperback.
ISBN: 0-87040-757-0

POP-UP GIFT CARDS by Masahiro Chatani
80 pp., 7 1/4 x 10 1/4 in., 16 pp. color, 64 pp. b/w photos and line drawings, paperback.
ISBN: 0-87040-768-6

POP-UP GEOMETRIC ORIGAMI by Masahiro Chatani and Keiko Nakazawa
86 pp., 7 1/4 x 10 1/4 in., 16 pp. color, 64 pp. b/w photos and line drawings, paperback.
ISBN: 0-87040-943-3

POP-UP ORIGAMIC ARCHITECTURE by Masahiro Chatani
88 pp., 7 1/4 x 10 1/4 in., 4 pp. color, 11 pp. b/w photos, 68 pp. line drawings, paperback.
ISBN: 0-87040-656-6

Quick & Easy ORIGAMI by Toshie Takahama
Boxed set, book: 60 pp.,, 6 x 6 in., 30 pp. color and 30 pp. line drawings, origami paper: 60 shetts in 6 colors.
ISBN: 4-88996-056-2

Quick & Easy ORIGAMI BOXES by Tomoko Fuse
Boxed set, book: 60 pp.,, 6 x 6 in., 30 pp. color and 30 pp. line drawings, origami paper: 60 shetts in 6 colors.
ISBN: 4-88996-052-X

SIMPLE TRADITIONAL ORIGAMI by Tomoko Fuse
80 pp., 7 1/4 x 10 1/4 in., 8 pp. color, 68 pp. 2 color line drawings, paperback.
ISBN: 4-88996-041-4

UNIT ORIGAMI: Multidimensional Transformations by Tomoko Fuse
244 pp., 7 1/4 x 10 1/4 in., 8 pp. color, 220 pp. b/w photos and line drawings, paperback.
ISBN: 0-87040-852-6

WORLD OF ORIGAMI, THE, by Isao Honda
182 pp., 8 1/4 x 11 3/4 in., 170 pp. b/w photos and line drawings, paperback.
ISBN: 0-87040-383-4